Sound of Living Waters

Sound of Living Waters:
Songs of the Spirit

Compiled by
BETTY PULKINGHAM
and
JEANNE HARPER

William B. Eerdmans Publishing Company
Grand Rapids, Michigan

Printed in the United States of America

reprinted 1976

First published 1974 by Hodder and Stoughton Limited, St. Paul's House, Warwick Lane, London. This American edition published by arrangement with Hodder and Stoughton.

Library of Congress Cataloging in Publication Data

Pulkingham, Betty, comp.
Sound of living waters : songs of renewal.

Hymns.
Includes indexes.
1. Hymns, English. I. Harper, Jeanne, joint comp.
II. Title.
M2198.P96S7 783.9'52 74-19456
ISBN 0-8028-1581-2 : (v. 1)

Cover design and illustrations
by Schumaker/Deur Designers, Inc.

Foreword

Sound of Living Waters is a book with many fresh sounds reflecting the cascade of joyous praise, of awesome wonder, of sincerity and hope, which accompany the Holy Spirit's renewal in the church today. It is not, strictly speaking, an innovative book; a great majority of the songs were chosen because of their proven usefulness in worship. In a sense our task as compilers has been not to choose, but to recognize what God seems already to have chosen. From the coasts of England, from the islands of New Zealand, from the expansive shores of America, the songs roll in as a powerful tide of praise to the Saviour. The ocean is deep and wide and so also is the musical scope of this book; it is not limited by period or style, not confined to youth or content with the old. Simply to turn a page may transport you from Handel to the sound of rock in *Godspell.* We believe that such a mixture of sounds reflects the wideness of God's mercy — like the wideness of the sea. Certainly it reflects the breadth and variety of sources from which the music has been drawn, because in a real sense the book represents many voices in many lands.

This is not a collection of songs by "experts," although Vaughan Williams and Bortniansky do have their say. So does a secretary named Sylvia, a young college student called Diane, and four-year-old David, son of one of the editors! The Holy Spirit gives songs as one means of encouraging the body of Christ, and the book you are holding would make an interesting manual for studying the creative process. There are songs here which are "open-ended"—verses may be added spontaneously—such as "Thank you, Lord" and "I will sing." Time-honored words may appear in new musical clothing: one such new hymn setting, "On Jordan's bank", was the result of a parish choir rehearsal to prepare for the Feast-day of St. John the Baptist. The song-gifts of the Holy Spirit may be evidenced in interesting and varied ways. In one English parish a simple bright chorus, "Thank you, thank you, Jesus," underwent a kind of metamorphosis: first, a member of the choir shared with the director his idea about the song ("I can hear it sung very slowly and worshipfully"). The director with some trepidation mentioned the seedling idea to the choir, and the following week a gifted young guitarist turned up with a unique reharmonization of the song expressive of quiet awe and wonder. Yet another chorister contributed a verse of words and gradually a new song emerged — a composite of many small parts yet woven into one unique whole. "The voice of God," said the prophet Ezekiel, "is as the sound of many waters." One sound . . . many waters.

Contents

1	Hallelujah! . . . Songs of praise and Thanksgiving	11
2	Kneel and Adore . . . Songs of Worship	39
3	Look Up . . . Songs of Hope and Vision	59
4	Become . . . Wholeness and Maturity	79
5	Songs of the Kingdom . . . The Body of Christ	95
6	Suffer — Reign . . . Songs of Faith and Victory	119
7	Go Forth . . . Outreach	145
8	Sing a Psalm	163
9	Come as Children . . . Songs for children of all ages	187
10	Songs for a Season	205
	INDEX OF TITLES AND FIRST LINES	241
	TOPICAL INDEX	243
	CHOIRMASTER'S GUIDE	247

Acknowledgments

The editors wish to acknowledge that there is one person without whose constant and diligent work this book would not have come to print. Mimi Farra, whose songs and musical arrangements are spotted throughout the book, has done a lion's share of the copying and preparation of the songs for engraving. The editors have relied heavily upon her sound musicianship and her precision-workmanship — and both have been available to us on a twenty-four hour basis — with a rare gift of encouragement thrown in for good measure! Perhaps the degree of her involvement can best be described in the words of nine-year-old Martha Pulkingham. When the new cover design for *Sound of Living Waters* was first seen at home, and the initial wave of approving comments had subsided, Martha's face was solemn and her brow furrowed. "Where," she announced in her gravest voice, "is *Mimi's* name?" . . . It is written invisibly on every page.

There are many others for whose help we are most grateful: to Nancy Newman and Oressa Wise, of Fisherman, Inc., for their able assistance with songs in the U.S.A.; to Pamela Thomson of Coventry, who allowed us frequent access to her quiet home and lovely piano, and brought us refreshments to help the work go faster; to John Waller and David Gardiner for their help as copyists; to many friends throughout Canada, U.S.A., England and New Zealand, who served as "song resource" personnel in our search for a truly representative selection of songs; and lastly to the saints at home who worked hard in order to set us free to turn our attention to the book, notably members of the Community of Celebration in Berkshire, and the members of the Harper household at 23 Spencer Road, East Molesey.

In the ebb and flow of music through the pages of this book is to be found not only variety but a certain unity characterized by gentleness and peaceful praise. Perhaps a few things need explaining. Most of the songs appear with guitar chords as well as simple piano accompaniments. When a song has neither of the above it is because we feel it can most effectively be sung by voices alone. The hymns and songs which lend themselves to part-singing are scored in traditional SATB (stems up and down) style. The *tempo* and expression markings appear at the heading of each song because we feel it matters how a song is sung! They sometimes describe the spirit of the song: triumphant, peaceful, joyful; at other times they give a practical clue as to its performance: well-accented, smoothly, lightly. The editors' suggestions in the footnotes are there because it is sometimes difficult to communicate in the black-and-whiteness of notes all that pertains to the character and potential of a song.

This is a songbook for people: for congregations, for prayer groups, for family gatherings. It is not oriented toward solo performances or trained choirs, yet you will find music suitable for both within its pages, and such songs have been indexed for your convenience. We hope you will peruse, enjoy and use this book, and since praise pleases our Father, we are confident that he too will enjoy this book — as you use it.

—*Betty Pulkingham and Jeanne Harper*

Hallelujah! . . . Songs of praise and Thanksgiving

1. Alleluia No. 1

Capo 3 (D)

Don Fishel
Arr. Betty Pulkingham

Rich and broad
Refrain
F(D)
Dm(Bm)
Gm(Em)
C(A)
Al-le - lu - ia, al-le - lu - ia, give thanks to the ris-en Lord. Al-le -
lu - ia, al-le - lu - ia, give praise to his name.
last time
Verses
B♭(G)
1. Je - sus is Lord of all the earth. He is the King of cre - a - tion.
2. Spread the good news o'er all the earth. Je - sus has died and has ris - en.
3. We have been cru - ci - fied with Christ. Now we shall live for ev - er.
Al - le -
name.

4. God has proclaimed the just reward,
Life for all men, alleluia.

5. Come let us praise the living God,
Joyfully sing to our Saviour.

2. The canticle of the gift

Capo 2 (Am)

Composer and author unknown
Arr. Betty Pulkingham

Joyfully, with a driving rhythm
Refrain
Bm(Am)
A(G)
Bm(Am)
O what a gift! What a won - der - ful gift! Who can
Em(Dm)
Bm(Am)
tell the won - ders of the Lord? Let us
A(G)
Bm(Am)
op - en our eyes, our ears, and our hearts; it is
A(G)
Bm(Am)
Christ the Lord, it is he!

Bm(Am)
1. In the still - ness of the night when the
2. On the night be - fore he died it was
3. On the hill of Cal - va - ry the
4. Ear - ly on that morn - ing when the
5. Some - day with the saints we will
A(G)
G(F)
A(G)
world was a - sleep, the al - migh - ty word leapt
Pass - ov - er night, and he gath - ered his friends to -
world held its breath, for there for the world to
guards were sleep - ing, back to life came
come be - fore our Fa - ther and then we will shout and dance and
Bm(Am)
out. He came to Ma - ry,
gether. He broke the bread,
see, God gave his Son, his
he! He con - quered death,
sing. For in our midst for our
A(G)
G(F)
A(G)
he came to us, Christ came to the land of Gal - i -
he blessed the wine; it was the gift of his love and his
ve - ry own Son for the love of you and ____
he con - quered sin, but the vic - t'ry he gave to you and
eyes to see will be Christ our Lord and our

Bm(Am)
F#m(Em)
Bm(Am)
Refrain
- lee.
life.
me.
me!
King.
Christ our Lord and our King!

3. Something in my heart

Anon.
Arr. Betty Pulkingham

Lightly and brightly

E E7 A E
Some - thing in my heart like a stream running free

F# B7
makes me feel so hap - py, as hap - py as can be;

E E7 A E
when I think of Je - sus and what he's done for me,

B7
E
some - thing in my heart like a stream run-ning free.

'Something in my heart' may be sung in sequence with the following:

4. Give me oil in my lamp

Anon.
Arr. Betty Pulkingham

Brightly

E
E7
A
1. Give me oil in my lamp, keep me burning. Give me

E
B7
oil in my lamp, I pray. Give me

E
E7
A
oil in my lamp, keep me burning, keep me

E
B7
E
burning 'til the break of day.
Refrain
E
E7
A
Sing ho-san - na, sing ho-san - na,
B7
1
E
A
E
2
E
sing ho-san-na to the King of Kings! King!

2. Make me a fisher of men, keep me seeking···
3. Give me joy in my heart, keep me singing···
4. Give me love in my heart, keep me serving···

Other verses may be added: Give me faith··· keep me praying; Give me peace··· keep me loving; *etc.*

5. Amazing grace

John Newton

Early American melody
Arr. Betty Pulkingham

Fervently

*G B7 C G G

1. A - ma - zing grace! How sweet the sound that saved a
3. Through ma - ny dan - gers, toils and snares, I have al -

A7 D G G7

wretch like me. ______ I once was lost, but
read - y come; ______ 'tis grace hath brought me

C G Em D G
now am found, was blind, but now I see.
safe thus far, and grace will lead me home.

G B7 C G
2. 'Twas grace that taught my heart to fear, and grace my
4. When we've been there ten thou - sand years, bright shin - ing
A7 D G G7
fears re - lieved. How pre - cious did that
as the sun, we've no less days to
C G Em D G
grace ap - pear the hour I first be - lieved.
sing God's praise than when we've first be - gun.

* Optional descant for 4th. verse is available by singing the top note in the piano part. Descant in bars 7 and 8 may remain on F sharp.

* Guitar chords are not designed to be used with harmonization of verses 1 and 3.

6. Oh! How good is the Lord

Anon.
Arr. Jeanne Harper

With joyful abandon
Refrain
A
E7
Oh! Oh! Oh! ___ how good is the Lord.
A
Oh! Oh! Oh! ___ how good is the Lord.
A7
D
Oh! Oh! Oh! ___ how good is the Lord. I
A
E7
A
Fine
ne - ver will for - get what he has done for me.

Verses
A
E7
1. He gives me sal – va – tion, how good is the Lord. He
A
gives me sal – va – tion, how good is the Lord. He
D
gives me sal – va – tion, how good is the Lord. I
A
E7
A
ne – ver will for – get what he has done for me.

2. He gives me his blessings ···
3. He gives me his Spirit ···
4. He gives me his healing ···
5. He gives me his glory ···

Other suitable verses may be added: He gives us each other ··· his body ··· his freedom, *etc.*

7. I will sing, I will sing

Max Dyer

Liltingly
I will sing, I will sing a song un - to the Lord. I will
Al - le - lu, al - le - lu - ia, glo - ry to the Lord. Al - le-
sing, I will sing a song un - to the Lord. I will
lu, al - le - lu - ia, glo - ry to the Lord. Al - le-
sing, I will sing a song un - to the Lord. Al - le-
lu, al - le - lu - ia, glo - ry to the Lord. Al - le-
lu - ia, glo - ry to the Lord.
lu - ia, glo - ry to the Lord.

Optional verses:

We will come, we will come as one before the Lord.
Alleluia, glory to the Lord.

If the Son, if the Son shall make you free,
you shall be free indeed.

They that sow in tears shall reap in joy.
Alleluia, glory to the Lord.

Ev'ry knee shall bow and ev'ry tongue confess
that Jesus Christ is Lord.

In his name, in his name we have the victory.
Alleluia, glory to the Lord.

This song is most effectively sung without any instrumental accompaniment, but with light clapping (finger tips of one hand on palm of another). Suggested rhythm: ♩ ♫♩ ♫♩, etc.

8. # Let us give thanks

Brian Howard
Arr. Betty Pulkingham

With driving rhythm, beginning softly and building throughout
Refrain
G C G
Let us give thanks
G C 1G 2G
that our names are writ-ten, writ-ten,
C G Am
writ-ten in the book of life, in-scribed up-on his
1G 2G verse 3
palms. palms.
Fine

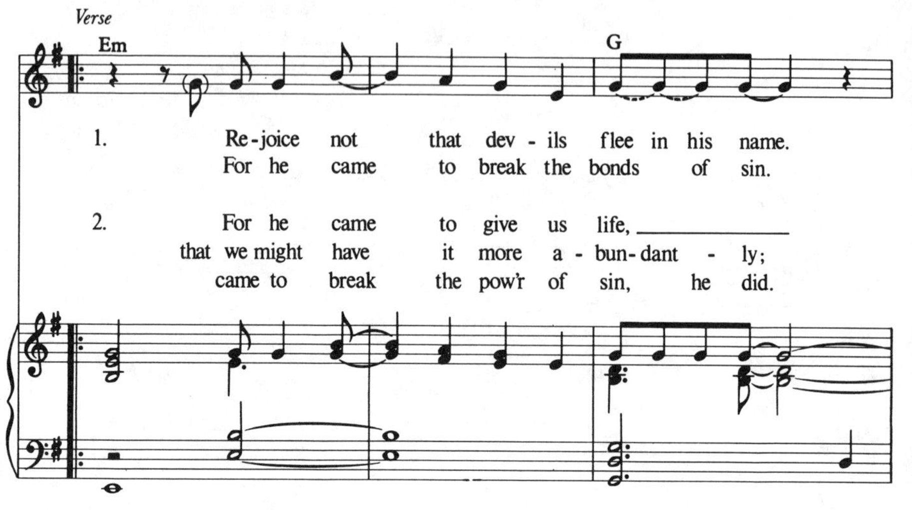
Verse
Em
G
1. Re-joice not that dev-ils flee in his name.
For he came to break the bonds of sin.
2. For he came to give us life,
that we might have it more a-bun-dant-ly;
came to break the pow'r of sin, he did.

no repeat v. 1
repeat twice v. 2
Em
Re-joice not in the pow-er
Yes, he did, he came to
Yes, he did, he came to

1 G
2 G
that he gave;
set us free, so

Refrain
verse 3 (voices only)
free - ly we sing.
Let ______ us give thanks,

thanks un - to the Fa - ther,

thanks un - to the Son,
thanks to the Ho - ly Spi

- rit,
our Lord God Three in One.
Refrain

Suggested clapping rhythm:

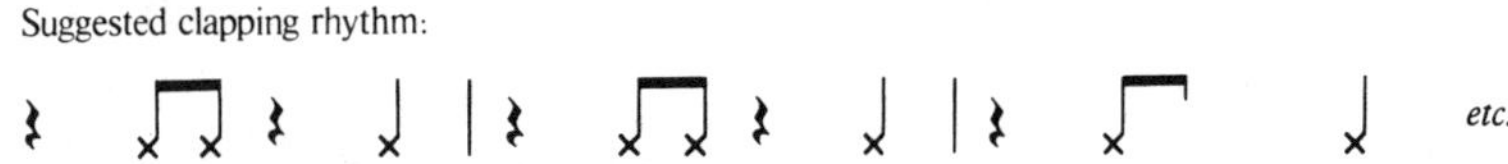
etc.

9. Morning has broken

Eleanor Farjeon

'Bunessan'
Old Gaelic melody
Arr. Betty Pulkingham

With an easy swing (1 beat to a bar)

1. Morn - ing has bro - ken like the first morn - ing; Black - bird has spo - ken like the first bird. Praise for the
2. Sweet the rain's new fall, sun - lit from heav - en, Like the first dew - fall on the first grass. Praise for the
3. Mine is the sun - light! Mine is the morn - ing; Born of the one light E - den saw play. Praise with e -

sing - ing! Praise for the morn - ing!
sweet - ness of the wet gar - den,
la - tion! Praise ev' ry morn - ing

Praise for them spring - ing fresh from the word.
Sprung in com - plete - ness where his feet pass.
God's re - cre - a - tion of the new day.

10. Rejoice in the Lord always

(2-Part round)

Capo 1 (E)

With a light, happy sound

Anon.

[1] F(E) C7(B7) F(E)
Re - joice in the Lord al - ways, and a - gain I say re - joice.

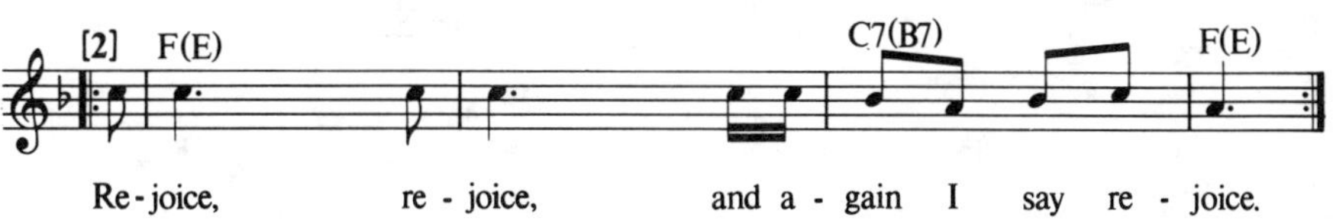

[2] F(E) C7(B7) F(E)
Re - joice, re - joice, and a - gain I say re - joice.

11.

Praise to the Lord

Joachim Neander
'Praise to the Lord'
The Chorale Book for England
Descant by Betty Pulkingham
Joyfully, with dignity
Descant
2. Praise to the Lord, he glo - rious - ly reign - eth; Borne as on ea - gle wings safe - ly sus - tain - eth.
4. Praise to the Lord, O let all a - dore him. All that hath breath join ___ now to a - dore him.
1. Praise to the Lord, the al - might - y, the King of cre - a - tion; O my soul, praise him, for he is thy health and sal - va - tion;
2. Praise to the Lord, o - ver all things he glo - rious - ly reign - eth; Borne as on ea - gle wings, safe - ly his saints he sus - tain - eth.
3. Praise to the Lord, who doth pros - per thy way and de - fend thee; Sure - ly his good - ness and mer - cy shall ev - ver at - tend thee;

Hast thou not seen How all thou
Let the a - men sum all our
Join the great throng, Psal - ter - y, or - gan and
Hast thou not seen How all thou need - est hath
Pon - der a - new What the al - might - y can
need - est hath been in what he or - dain - eth.
prais - es a - gain as we wor - ship be - fore him.
song, Sound - ing in glad a - do - ra - tion.
been Gran - ted in what he or - dain - eth?
do, Who with his love doth be - friend thee.

4. Praise to the Lord! O let all that is in me adore him!
All that hath breath join with Abraham's seed to adore him!
Let the 'Amen'
Sum all our praises again
Now as we worship before him.

12. # Angel voices ever singing

Francis Pott

'Maiquez'
Geoffrey Beaumont

Smoothly
1. An - gel voi - ces ev - er sing - ing Round thy throne of light, Angel harps for ev - er ring - ing, Rest not day nor night; Thou-sands on - ly live to bless thee, And con-fess thee Lord of might. thee.
2. Thou who art be - yond the far - thest Mor - tal eye can scan. Can it be that thou re - gard - est Songs of sin - ful man? Can we know that thou art near us And wilt hear us? Yes, we can.
3. Yes, we know that thou re - joic - est O'er each work of thine; Thou didst ears and hands and voi - ces For thy praise de - sign; Craftsman's art and mu - sic's mea - sure For thy plea - sure All com - bine.
1-4
last verse

From 'Thirty 20th. Century Hymn Tunes'

4. In thy house, great God, we offer
Of thine own to thee;
And for thine acceptance proffer
All unworthily,
Hearts and minds and hands and voices
In our choicest
Psalmody.

5. Honour, glory, might, and merit
Thine shall ever be,
Father, Son and Holy Spirit,
Blessed Trinity.
Of the best that thou hast given
Earth and heaven
Render thee.

13. This is the day

Fiji Island Folk Melody

1. This is the day, this is the day that the Lord has made, that the
Lord has made. We will re-joice, we will re-joice and be
glad in it, and be glad in it. This is the day that the Lord has made.
We will re-joice and be glad in it.
This is the day that the Lord hath made.

2. This is the day when he rose again.
3. This is the day when the Spirit came.

14. Praise him

Anon.
Arr. Jeanne Harper

Smoothly, without dragging
E
B7
E
E7
1. Praise him, praise him,
A
E
praise him in the morn - ing, praise him in the noon - time,
B7
C#m
praise him, praise him,
E
B7
E
praise him when the sun goes down.

2. Jesus... 3. Love him ... 4. Trust him ... 5. Serve him ...

15. Hallelujah! Jesus is Lord!

Adapted from Rev. 7 — Mimi Farra

With rhythmic boldness
Refrain
A G A G Em A
Hal - le - lu - jah! Hal - le - lu - jah!
Hal - le - lu - jah! Je - sus is (1) Lord!
(2) King!
Verses
D A Em A
1. All gath - er round the ___ throne of the Lamb,
2. Lift up your voice with the thousands who cry:
3. Bless - ing and hon - or and glo - ry and pow'r
D A Em A
his prais - es sing through - out e - ter - ni - ty.
'Wor - thy, wor - thy art thou, Lamb of God.'
be un - to him ___ for - ev - er and ev - er.

4. All glory be to the one Triune God,
The Father, Son, and the (𝄽) Holy Spirit.

16. Jesus Christ is alive today

Anon.
Arr. Betty Pulkingham

Boldly
A
D
Je - sus Christ is a - live to - day,
I
we
A
E
know
I
we
know it's true.
A
D
Sov' - reign of the un - i - verse,
I
we
A
E7
A
A7
give him hom - age due.

D
A
Seat - ed there at God's right hand,
B7
E
I am
we are
with him in the pro - mised land.
A
D
Je - sus lives and reigns in
me,
you,
that's
A
E7
A
how I know it's true.

17. O for a thousand tongues

Charles Wesley

'Lyngham'
Thomas Jarman

Joyfully, with movement
1. O for a thou - sand tongues to sing My
2. Je - sus! the name that charms our fears, That
3. He breaks the power of can - celled sin, He
great re - deem - er's praise, my great re - deem - er's praise,
bids our sor - rows cease, that bids our sor - rows cease;
sets the pris - oner free, he sets the pris - oner free;
The glo - ries of my God and King, The
'Tis mu - sic in the sin - ner's ears, 'Tis
His blood can make the foul - est clean, His
1. The tri-umphs of his

tri - umphs of his grace, The tri - umphs of his
life, and health, and peace, 'Tis life, and health, and
blood a - vailed for me, His blood a - vailed for
grace, The tri - umphs of his grace, The
grace, The tri - umphs of his grace!
peace, 'Tis life, and health, and peace.
me, His blood a - vailed for me.
tri - umphs of his grace, The tri - umphs of his grace!

4. He speaks, and, listening to his voice,
   New life the dead receive,
   The mournful, broken hearts rejoice,
   The humble poor believe.

5. Hear him, ye deaf; his praise, ye dumb,
   Your loosened tongues employ;
   Ye blind, behold your Saviour come;
   And leap, ye lame, for joy!

6. My gracious master and my God,
   Assist me to proclaim,
   To spread through all the earth abroad
   The honours of thy name.

18. Thank you, thank you, Jesus

Anon.
Arr. Betty Pulkingham

Cheerfully
E
A
E
1. Thank you, thank you, Je - sus. Thank you, thank you, Je - sus.
B7
Thank you, thank you, Je - sus, in my heart.
E
E7
A
E
Thank you, thank you, Je - sus. Oh, thank you, thank you, Je - sus.
B7
E
Thank you, thank you, Je - sus, in my heart.

2. You can't make me doubt him. *(repeat)*
   You can't make me doubt him in my heart.
   You can't make me doubt him. *(repeat)*
   Thank you, thank you, Jesus, in my heart.

3. I can't live without him. *(repeat)*
   I can't live without him in my heart.
   I can't live without him. *(repeat)*
   Thank you, thank you, Jesus, in my heart.

4. Glory, hallelujah! *(repeat)*
   Glory, hallelujah, in my heart!
   Glory, hallelujah! *(repeat)*
   Thank you, thank you, Jesus, in my heart!

Kneel and Adore . . .
Songs of Worship

19. Holy, holy

Jimmy Owens

Reverently
C Em/B Dm/A G7 C Em7/B Am7 C/G
melody
(Unison) 1. Ho - ly, ho - ly, ho - ly,
Dm7 G Dm7 G7
ho - ly. Ho - ly, ho - ly, Lord God Al -
C C7 F F/E Dm7 D♯dim7
melody
migh - ty; And we lift our hearts be-fore you as a

C
E
Em7
Am
Dm7
G7
melody
tok - en of our love, Ho - ly, ho - ly, ho ly,
1-5
C
Dm7
G7
6
C
rit.
C
ho - ly. 2. Gra - cious
lu jah.
rit.

Any of the following may be sung in parts:

2. Gracious Father, gracious Father,
We're so glad to be your children, gracious Father;
And we lift our heads before you as a token of our love,
Gracious Father, gracious Father.

3. Precious Jesus, precious Jesus,
We're so glad that you've redeemed us, precious Jesus,
And we lift our hands before you as a token of our love,
Precious Jesus, precious Jesus.

4. Holy Spirit, Holy Spirit,
Come and fill our hearts anew, Holy Spirit,
And we lift our voice before you as a token of our love,
Holy Spirit, Holy Spirit.

5. Holy, holy, *(same as verse 1)*

6. Hallelujah, hallelujah, hallelujah, hallelujah,
And we lift our hearts before you as a token of our love,
Hallelujah, hallelujah.

20. Let all that is within me

Capo 1(E)

Anon.
Arr. Betty Pulkingham

Freely
F(E)
C 7(B7)
Let all that is with-in me cry, 'Ho - ly.'
Let all that is with-in me cry,
F(E)
'Ho - ly.'
Ho - ly,
B♭(A)
F(E)
B♭(A)
F(E)
C7(B7)
F(E)
Ho - ly, Ho - ly is the Lamb that was slain.

Let all that is within me cry, 'Worthy'... 'Jesus'... 'glory'

21. Son of God

Oressa Wise
With unhurried simplicity
C G7 C
1. & 4. Son of God, Son of God, we come be-fore you to love and a-dore you, Son of God.
2. Word of God, Word of God, we come to hear you, to al - ways be near you, Word of God.
3. Lamb of God, Lamb of God, we come to bless you, to ev - er con-fess you, Lamb of God.
F C F C G7 C G7 C

22. God himself is with us

Gerhardt Tersteegen

'Tysk'
German melody

Reverently
1. God him - self is with us; Let us all a - dore him,
2. Come, a - bide with - in me; Let my soul, like Ma - ry,
3. Glad - ly we sur - ren - der Earth's de - ceit - ful trea - sures,
And with awe ap - pear be - fore him. God is here with -
Be thine earth - ly sanc - tu - a - ry. Come, in - dwell - ing
Pride of life, and sin - ful plea - sures: Glad - ly, Lord, we
in us: Soul, in si - lence fear him, Hum - bly, fer - vent -
Spi - rit, With trans - fig - ured splen - dor; Love and hon - or
of - fer Thine to be for ev - er, Soul and life and

-ly draw near him. Now his own who have known
will I ren - der. Where I go here be - low,
each en - deav - or. Thou a - lone shalt be known
God, in wor - ship low - ly, Yield their spi - rits whol - ly.
Let me bow be - fore thee, Know thee, and a - dore thee.
Lord of all our be - ing, Life's true way de - cree - ing.

23. We see the Lord

Isaiah 6:1

Anon.
Arr. Betty Pulkingham

Sung slowly in quiet adoration

E
E *Descant*
We see Je - sus.
We see the Lord,

We see Je - sus.
We see the Lord, And he is

B7
E
High, he is high,
high and lift - ed up, And his train fills the tem-ple. He is

B7
E
he is high.
high and lift-ed up, And his train fills the tem-ple. The
A E
A E
An-gels cry, 'Ho ly,' The an-gels cry, 'Ho-ly,' The
an-gels cry, 'Ho-ly,' The an-gels cry, 'Ho-ly,' The
B7
E
A
E
an-gels cry, 'Ho-ly is the Lord.'
an-gels cry, 'Ho-ly is the Lord.'

24. He is Lord

Anon.
Arr. Betty Pulkingham

Broad and full

B7
E
He is Lord, he is Lord. He is
F♯
B7
ris - en from the dead, and he is Lord. Ev' - ry
E
E7
A
F♯m
knee shall bow, ev' - ry tongue con - fess that
E
B7
E
Je - sus Christ is Lord.

25. Alleluia

Anon.
Arr. Betty Pulkingham

With quiet adoration

G
C
Am
1. Al - le - lu - ia, Al - le - lu - ia, Al - le -
D
1C G
2C G
lu - ia, Al - le - lu - ia, Al - le - lu - ia.

2. How I love him 3. Blessed Jesus 4. My Redeemer 5. Jesus is Lord 6. Alleluia

26. Father, we adore you

(3-part round)

Capo 1 (E)

Terrye Coelho

Slowly, sustained

1 F(E) Gm(F#m) C(B7) F(E) 2 Gm(F#m) C(B7) F(E) 3 Gm(F#m) C(B7) F(E)
1. Fa - ther
2. Je - sus
3. Spi - rit
we a - dore you; lay our lives be - fore you. How we love you.

27. Thank you, thank you, Jesus

Anon.
Arr. St. Philip's Church, Coventry
Harm. Richard Gullen

Slowly, with deep feeling
E
AM7 E E7
A
1. Thank you, thank you, Jesus. Thank you, thank you,
F#m G#m
C#m
G#m F#m
Jesus. Oh, thank you, thank you, Jesus in my
B7
E
heart. Thank you, thank you,
AM7 E E7
A
F#m G#m
Jesus. Oh, thank you, thank you, Jesus. Oh,

C#m
G#m
F#m B7
E
thank you, thank you, Je - sus, in my heart.
1-3
final ending

2. Love you, love you, Jesus. *(repeat)*
Oh, love you, love you, Jesus, in my heart.

3. Father, God almighty; *(repeat)*
Oh, Father, God almighty, take my heart.

4. Glory hallelujah! *(repeat)*
Oh, glory hallelujah in my heart.

28. Thou art worthy

Rev. 4: 11 and 5: 9,10.
Verse 2 - Tom Smail

Pauline Michael Mills

Reverently
1. Thou art wor - thy, thou art wor - thy,
2. Thou art wor - thy, thou art wor - thy,
thou art wor - thy, O Lord.
thou art wor - thy, O Lamb.
Thou art wor - thy, to re - ceive glo - ry,
Thou art wor - thy, to re - ceive glo - ry, and
glo - ry and hon - our and power. For
power at the Fa - ther's right hand. For

thou hast cre - a - ted, hast all things cre - a - ted, for
thou hast re - deemed us, hast ran - somed and cleaned us
thou hast cre - a - ted all things.
by thy blood set - ting us free. In
And for thy plea - sure they are cre - a - ted;
white robes arr - ayed us, kings and priests made us, And
thou art wor - thy, O Lord.
we are reign - ing in thee.

29. Spirit of the living God

Capo 3 (D)

Daniel Iverson
Arr. Betty Pulkingham
Unhurried, with a rich sound
Spi - rit of the liv - ing God, fall a-fresh on me.
Spi - rit of the liv - ing God, fall fresh on me.
Break me, melt me, mould me, fill me.
Spi - rit of the liv - ing God, fall a-fresh on me.

30. Jesus, never have I heard a name

Anon.
Arr. Betty Pulkingham

Tenderly
Je - sus, Je - sus, Je - sus,
1
nev - er have I heard a name that thrills my soul like thine.
2
oh, what match - less grace that links that pre - cious name with mine.

32. Jesus, Jesus, wonderful Lord

Capo 3 (G)

Sylvia Lawton

Tenderly and with warmth

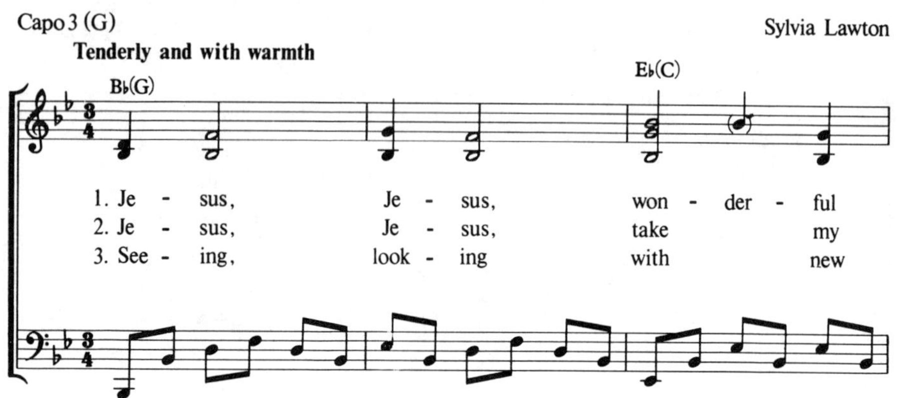

B♭(G)
E♭(C)
1. Je - sus, Je - sus, won - der - ful
2. Je - sus, Je - sus, take my
3. See - ing, look - ing with new

B♭(G)
Lord. Gen - tly you touched me and
life. Je - sus, Je - sus,
eyes; lov - ing, car - ing

Cm(Am)
F7(D7)
B♭(G)
made my life whole; how can I
I give to you, all things,
just as you do; learn - ing

Song number 31 has been deleted from this edition inasmuch as the copyright holder has declined to grant the publishers permission for its continued use.

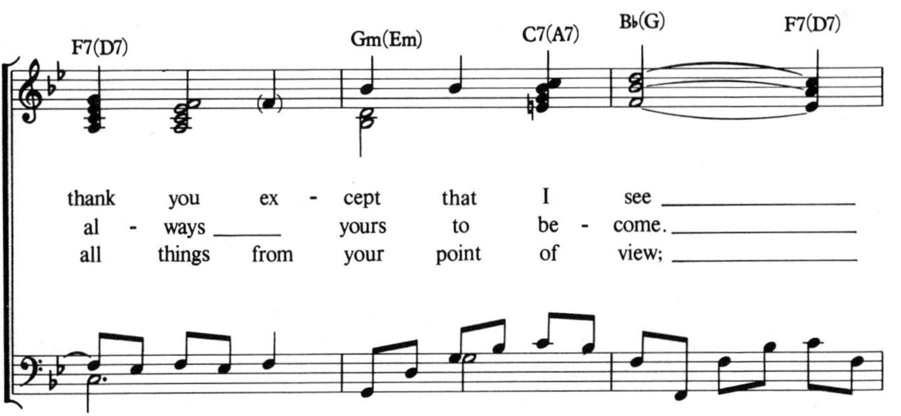
F7(D7)
Gm(Em)
C7(A7)
B♭(G)
F7(D7)
thank you ex - cept that I see
al - ways yours to be - come.
all things from your point of view;

E♭(C)
B♭(G)
F7(D7)
B♭(G)
your way of life is tru - ly for me?
Je - sus my Sav - iour, I will be thine.
Lord Je - sus Christ, your touch is so true.

33. Spirit divine

Andrew Reed

'Graefenberg'
Johann Crueger

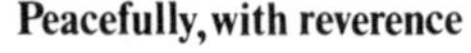
Peacefully, with reverence

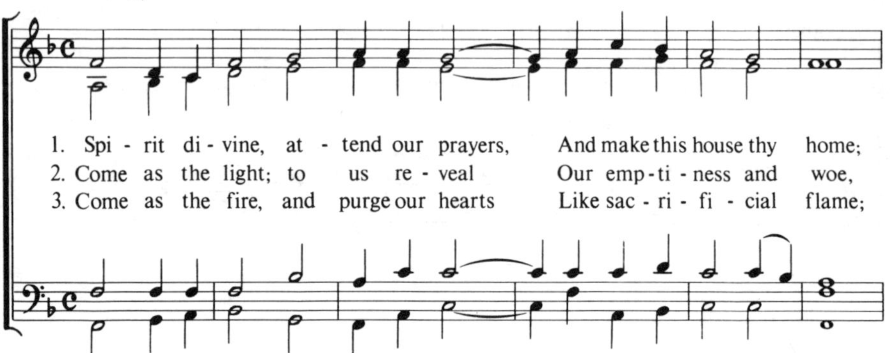
1. Spi - rit di - vine, at - tend our prayers, And make this house thy home;
2. Come as the light; to us re - veal Our emp - ti - ness and woe,
3. Come as the fire, and purge our hearts Like sac - ri - fi - cial flame;

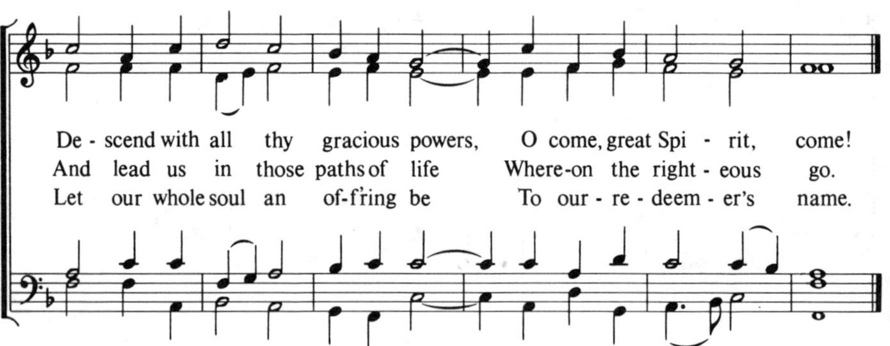
De - scend with all thy gracious powers, O come, great Spi - rit, come!
And lead us in those paths of life Where-on the right - eous go.
Let our whole soul an of-f'ring be To our - re - deem - er's name.

4. Come as the dove, and spread thy wings,
The wings of peaceful love;
And let thy Church on earth become
Blest as the Church above.

5. Spirit divine, attend our prayers;
Make a lost world thy home;
Descend with all thy gracious powers;
O come, great Spirit, come!

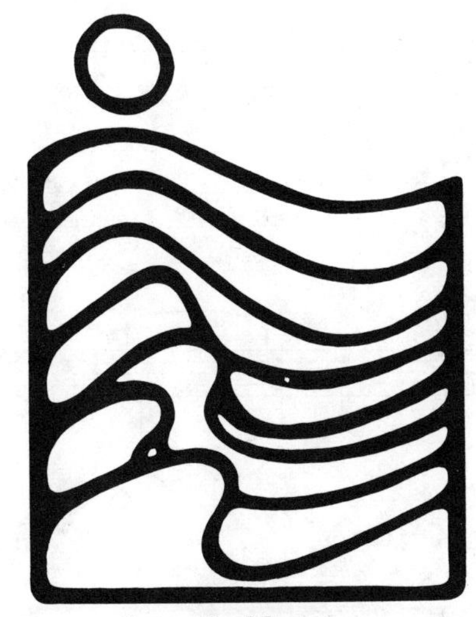

Look Up . . .
Songs of Hope and Vision

34. I want to walk as a child of the light

Kathleen Thomerson

Richly

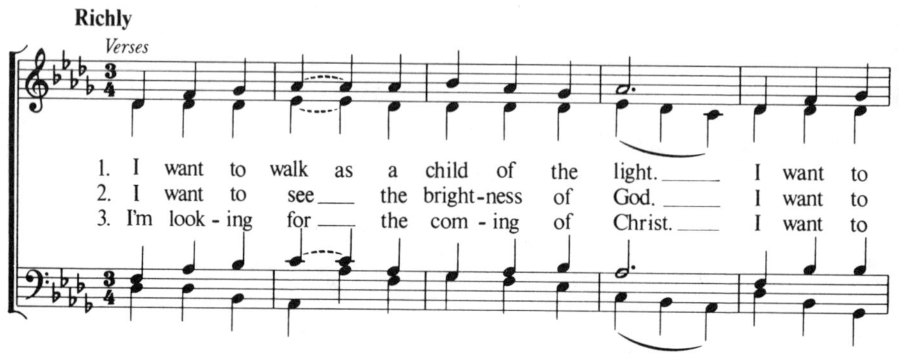
Verses
1. I want to walk as a child of the light. I want to
2. I want to see the bright-ness of God. I want to
3. I'm look - ing for the com - ing of Christ. I want to

fol - low Je - sus. God set the stars to give
look at Je - sus. Clear sun of righteous - ness,
be with Je - sus. When we have run with

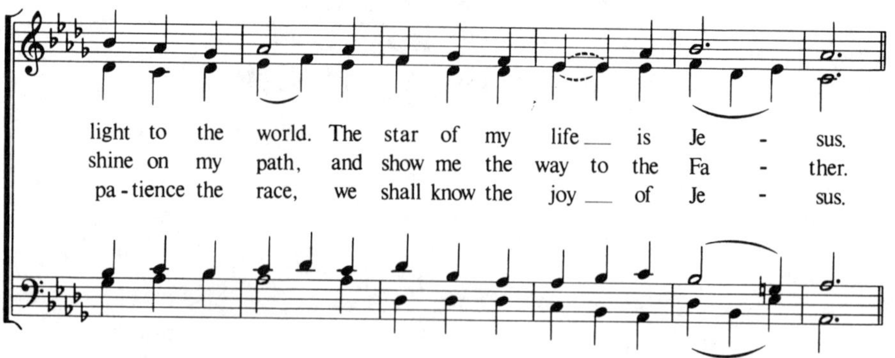
light to the world. The star of my life is Je - sus.
shine on my path, and show me the way to the Fa - ther.
pa - tience the race, we shall know the joy of Je - sus.

Refrain
In him there is no dark - ness at all, the
night and the day are both a - like. The
rit.
Lamb is the light of the cit - y of God.
a tempo
Shine in my heart, Lord Je - sus.

35. In Christ there is no east or west

John Oxenham

North American spiritual
Arr. Betty Pulkingham

With breadth
A
E
G
D
1. In Christ there is no east or west, In
2. In him shall true hearts ev - 'ry - where Their
3. Join hands then, broth - ers of the faith, What -
Bm
E
A
D
A
F#m
Bm7
him no south or north, But one great fel - low -
high com - mun - ion find; His ser - vice is the
e'er your race may be; Who serves my Fa - ther
E
F#m
A
E7
A
- ship of love Through-out the whole wide earth.
gold - en cord Close bind - ing all man - kind.
as a son Is sure - ly kin to me.

4. In Christ now meet both east and west,
   In him meet south and north.
All Christly souls are one in him
   Throughout the whole wide earth.

36. Lord, I want to be a Christian

American folk hymn
Arr. Betty Pulkingham

Thoughtfully, not fast
D A D G
1. Lord, I want to be a Christian, in-a my heart, in-a my
D A Bm G D G
heart. Lord, I want to be a Christian in-a my heart, (in-a my
D G D
heart,) in-a my heart, (in-a my heart,) in-a my heart, (in-a my
Bm G D
heart.) Lord, I want to be a Christian in-a my heart.

2. Lord, I want to be more loving etc.
3. Lord, I want to be like Jesus etc.
4. Lord, I want to praise you freely etc.

37. Day by day

Richard of Chichester
Verse 2 - Jeanne Harper
D. Austin
Gently
F Gm C7 F Dm G7
1. Day by day, dear Lord, of thee three things I
2. Day by day, dear Lord, of thee three things I
C7 F D7 G Gm7
pray: to see thee more clear - ly, to love thee more
pray: to trust thee more full - ly, to leave things more
C C7 F B♭6 F C7 F
dear - ly, to fol - low thee more near - ly day by day.
whol - ly, to lean on thee se - cure - ly day by day.

38. Day by day

'Godspell'

Stephen Schwartz
Easy waltz feel
FM7
Gm7
FM7
Day by day,
Gm7
FM7
Gm7
Day by day,
B♭M7
Am7
Gm7
O dear Lord, three things I pray:
3
Em7
A7
To see thee more clear - ly,

Em7 A7 Dm G

love thee more dear - ly, Fol-low thee more near - ly,

1 CM7 2 CM7 *light rock feeling (faster)*

day by day, day by day.

Optional descant
FM7
Gm7
FM7
Day by day,
Day by day,
Day by day,

Gm7
B♭M7
Am7
Day by day,
O dear Lord, three
GM7
Em
Three things I pray
Melody in alto
things I pray,
To see thee more

A
Em
A
Day by day, ___
Day by day_
clear - ly,
Love thee more
dear - ly (Fol - low
Love thee more dear - ly,
dear - ly,
Dm
G
1 CM7
thee.) Fol-low thee more
near - ly,
day by day. ___

2
CM7
FM7
Day by day,
CM7
FM7
AM7
Day by day by day by day by day by day.

39. Reach out and touch the Lord

Capo 1 (E)

Bill Harmon

Simply
F(E)
Bb(A)
F(E)
Reach out and touch the Lord as he goes by. You'll
G(F#)
C7(B7)
find he's not too bus - y to hear your heart's cry. He's
F(E)
Bb(A)
F(E)
pass - ing by this mo - ment your needs to sup - ply. Reach
F6/4(E B bass)
C7(B7)
F(E)
out and touch the Lord as he goes by.

40. I want to live for Jesus every day

Anon.
Arr. Jeanne Harper

Brightly
C
G7
I want to live for Je - sus ev' - ry day. (ev' - ry day)
sim.
C
I want to live for Je - sus, come what may. (come what may)
F
C
A7
Take the world and all its plea - sure, I've got a more en - dur - ing trea - sure.
Dm
G7
C
I want to live for Je - sus ev' - ry day.

2. I'm gonna' live for Jesus ev'ry day *etc.*

41. He shall teach you all things

(for unison voices with optional canon)

Philip Humphreys

Gently, repeat ad lib.
Part 1
Part 2
Piano
He shall teach you all things, He shall teach you all things, and bring all things to your re-mem-brance, and bring all
(mem - brance) He shall teach you all things, He shall teach you all things, and bring all things to your re-mem-brance, and

things to your re - mem brance.
bring all things to your re -
rit.
mem brance.
rit.
42.
Kum ba yah
('Come by here')
Quietly
Traditional Spiritual
Kum ba yah, my Lord, Kum ba yah, Kum ba yah, my Lord, Kum ba yah, Kum ba
yah, my Lord, Kum ba yah, O Lord, Kum ba yah.

2 Someone's crying, Lord, Kum ba yah…
3 Someone's singing, Lord, Kum ba yah…
4 Someone's praying, Lord, Kum ba yah…

(Other intercessory verses may be added.. Someone's hungry. .lonely. .wounded. .dying, *etc.*)

43. O Breath of Life

Bessie Porter Head

'Spiritus Vitae'
Mary J. Hammond

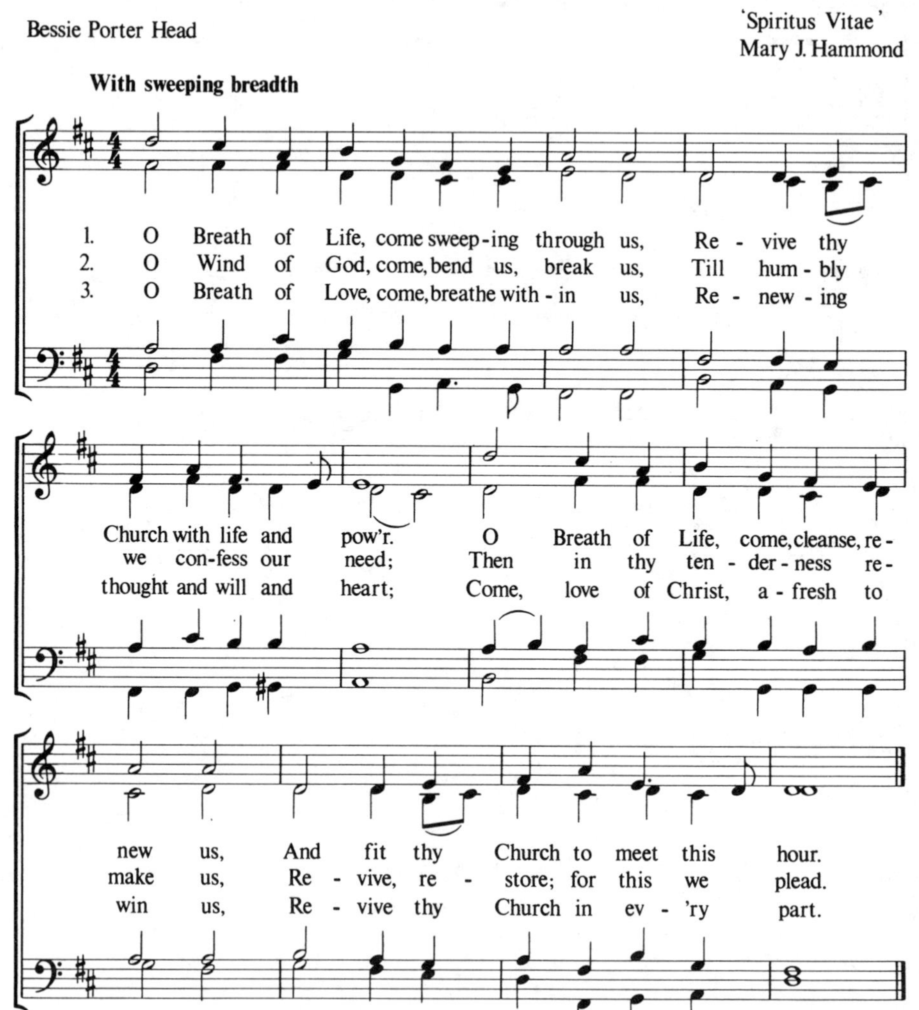
With sweeping breadth
1. O Breath of Life, come sweep-ing through us, Re - vive thy Church with life and pow'r. O Breath of Life, come, cleanse, re - new us, And fit thy Church to meet this hour.
2. O Wind of God, come, bend us, break us, Till hum - bly we con-fess our need; Then in thy ten - der - ness re - make us, Re - vive, re - store; for this we plead.
3. O Breath of Love, come, breathe with - in us, Re - new - ing thought and will and heart; Come, love of Christ, a - fresh to win us, Re - vive thy Church in ev - 'ry part.

4. Revive us, Lord! Is zeal abating
While harvest fields are vast and white?
Revive us, Lord, the world is waiting,
Equip thy Church to spread the light.

44. Lord of all hopefulness

Capo 1 (D)
Jan Struther

'Slane'
Traditional Irish melody

In unison, with movement
D A7 D D
1. Lord of all hope-ful-ness, Lord of all joy, Whose
2. Lord of all ea-ger-ness, Lord of all faith, Whose
3. Lord of all kind-li-ness, Lord of all grace, Your
A Em G A
trust, ev-er child-like, no cares could des-troy, Be
strong hands were skilled at the plane and the lathe, Be
hands swift to wel-come, your arms to em-brace, Be
G D Bm7 G A
there at our wa-king, and give us, we pray, Your
there at our la-bors, and givé us, we pray, Your
there at our ho-ming, and give us, we pray, Your
D Bm7 Em Em7 D
bliss in our hearts, Lord, at the break of the day.
strength in our hearts, Lord, at the noon of the day.
love in our hearts, Lord, at the eve of the day.

4. Lord of all gentleness, Lord of all calm,
Whose voice is contentment, whose presence is balm,
Be there at our sleeping, and give us, we pray,
Your peace in our hearts, Lord, at the end of the day.

45. At the name of Jesus

Caroline M. Noel

'King's Weston'
Ralph Vaughan Williams
Descant by
Betty Pulkingham

In unison, with vigor

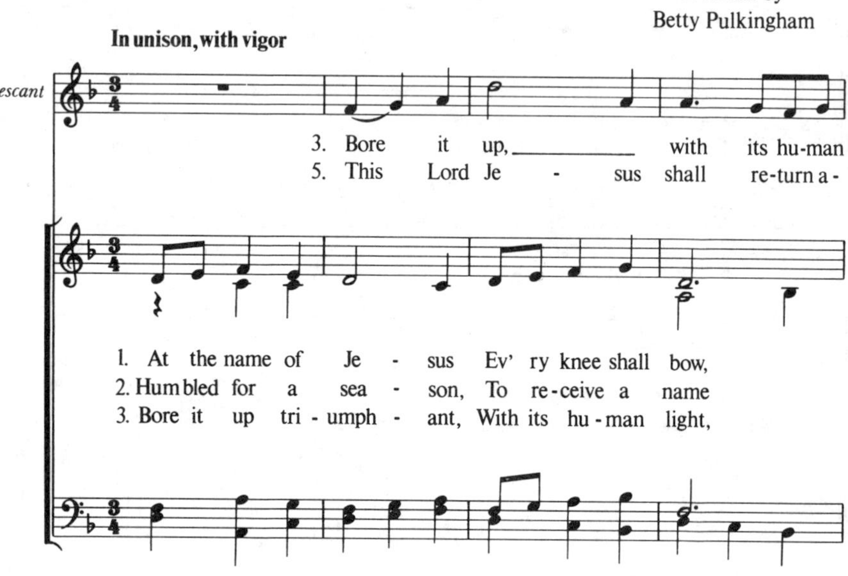

Descant
3. Bore it up, with its hu-man
5. This Lord Je - sus shall re-turn a-
1. At the name of Je - sus Ev' ry knee shall bow,
2. Hum bled for a sea - son, To re-ceive a name
3. Bore it up tri - umph - ant, With its hu - man light,

light through all ranks of crea - tures, to the cen - tral
-gain, with his Fa - ther's glo - ry o'er the earth to
Ev' - ry tongue con - fess him King of glo - ry now.
From the lips of sin - ners, Un - to whom he came,
Through all ranks of crea - tures, To the cen - tral height,

From 'Enlarged Songs of Praise' by permission of Oxford University Press.

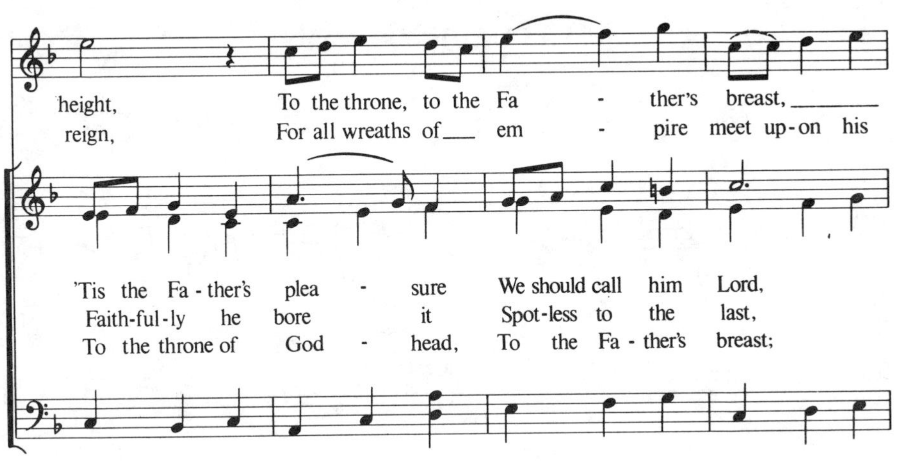
height, To the throne, to the Fa - ther's breast, ___
reign, For all wreaths of ___ em - pire meet up-on his
'Tis the Fa-ther's plea - sure We should call him Lord,
Faith-ful-ly he bore it Spot-less to the last,
To the throne of God - head, To the Fa-ther's breast;

Filled ___ it with the glo-ry of that per - fect rest.
brow, and our hearts con-fess him King of glo - ry now.
Who from the be-gin - ing Was the migh - ty Word.
Brought it back vic-to - rious, When from death he passed;
Filled it with the glo - ry Of that per - fect rest.

4. In your hearts enthrone him:
   There let him subdue
All that is not holy,
   All that is not true:
Crown him as your captain
   In temptation's hour;
Let his will enfold you
   In its light and power.

5. Brothers, this Lord Jesus
   Shall return again,
With his Father's glory
   O'er the earth to reign;
For all wreaths of empire
   Meet upon his brow,
And our hearts confess him
   King of glory now.

46. At the name of Jesus

Caroline M. Noel

'Camberwell'
John M. Brierley

1-4
Last Verse
p

Become . . .
Wholeness and Maturity

47. I want to walk with Jesus Christ

St. Paul's Erith 1964 Houseparty

Swiss folk tune
Arr. Betty Pulkingham

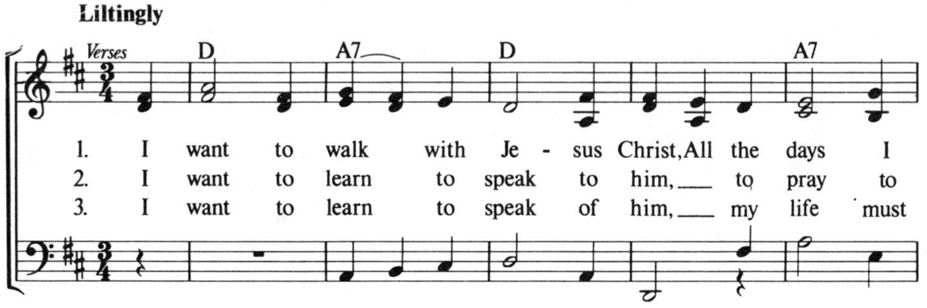

Liltingly
Verses
D
A7
D
A7
1. I want to walk with Je - sus Christ, All the days I
2. I want to learn to speak to him, to pray to
3. I want to learn to speak of him, my life must

D
G
live of this life on earth, To give to him com -
him, con - fess my sin, To op - en my life and
show that he lives in me. My deeds, my thoughts, my

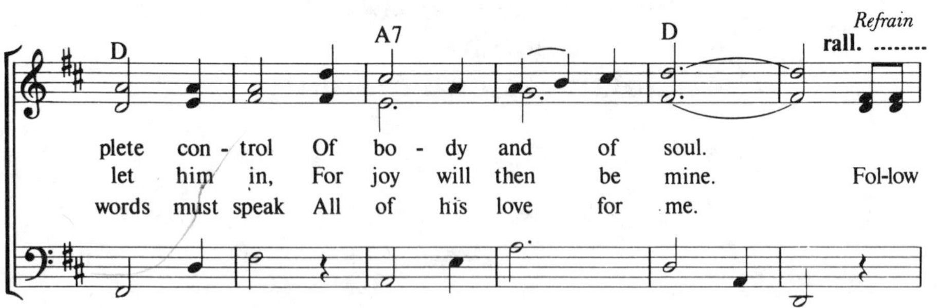

D
A7
D
Refrain
rall.
plete con - trol Of bo - dy and of soul.
let him in, For joy will then be mine. Fol-low
words must speak All of his love for me.

A7
D
a tempo, well accented
A7
him, fol-low him, yield your life to him, he has con - quered

D
G
death, he is king of kings. Ac - cept the joy which he

D
A7
D
gives to those who yield their lives to him.

4. I want to learn to read his word,
   For this is how I know the way
   To live my life as pleases him,
   In holiness and joy.

5. O Holy Spirit of the Lord,
   Enter now into this heart of mine,
   Take full control of my selfish will
   And make me wholly thine.

48. How sweet the name of Jesus sounds

John Newton

Gary Miles

Tenderly, in unison
G
Am
C
3
G
1. How sweet the name of Je - sus sounds In a be-
2. It makes the wound - ed spi - rit whole, And calms the
3. Dear name, the rock on which I build, My shield and

Bm7
CM7
D
Em
C
3
liev - er's ear! It soothes his sor - rows, heals his
trou - bled breast; 'Tis man - na to the hun - gry
hid - ing place, My nev - er - fail - ing treas - 'ry,

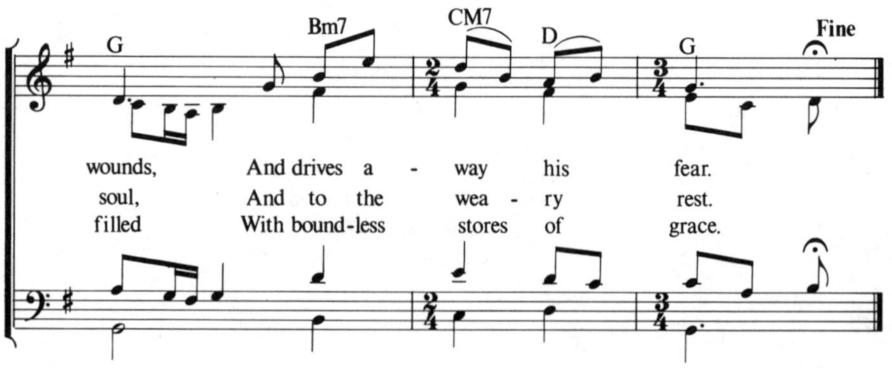

G
Bm7
CM7
D
G
Fine
wounds, And drives a - way his fear.
soul, And to the wea - ry rest.
filled With bound-less stores of grace.

4. Jesus! my Shepherd, Brother, Friend,
 My Prophet, Priest, and King,
My Lord, my Life, my Way, my End,
 Accept the praise I bring.

5. Weak is the effort of my heart,
 And cold my warmest thought;
But when I see thee as thou art,
 I'll praise thee as I ought.

6. Till then I would thy love proclaim
 With every fleeting breath;
And may the music of thy name
 Refresh my soul in death.

Optional interlude

49. # Here comes Jesus

Anon.
Arr. Betty Pulkingham

Slowly
C
Here comes Je - sus, see him walk-ing on the
F
wa - ter,
he'll lift you up
C
and he'll help you to
G7
stand.
Here comes
C
Je - sus,
he's the master of the waves
F
that roll.

C
G7
C
Here comes Je - sus, he'll make you whole.
Moving ahead faster
A7
D
Here comes Je - sus, see him walk-ing on the
G
D
wa - ter, he'll lift you up and he'll help you to
A7
D
stand. Here comes Je - sus,

G
he's the master of the waves that roll.
Here comes
D
A7
D
Je - sus,
he'll make you whole.
Still faster!
B7
E
Here comes Je - sus,
see him walk-ing on the
A
E
wa - ter, he'll lift you up
and he'll help you to

B7
E
stand. Here comes Je - sus,
A
he's the master of the waves that roll. Here comes
Broad and slow
E
B7
E
A
E
A
Je - sus, he'll make you whole. Here comes
E
B7
E
A
E
Je - sus, he'll save your soul.

50. Silver and gold have I none

Anon.
Arr. Betty Pulkingham

Rollicking

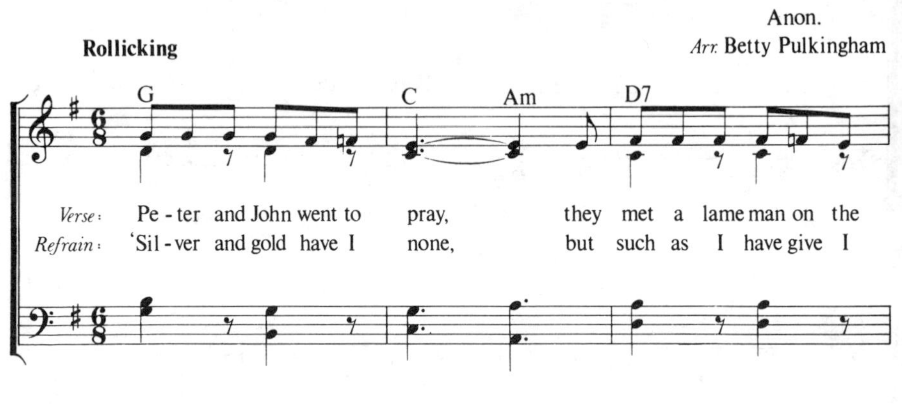
G
C
Am
D7
Verse: Pe - ter and John went to pray, they met a lame man on the
Refrain: 'Sil - ver and gold have I none, but such as I have give I

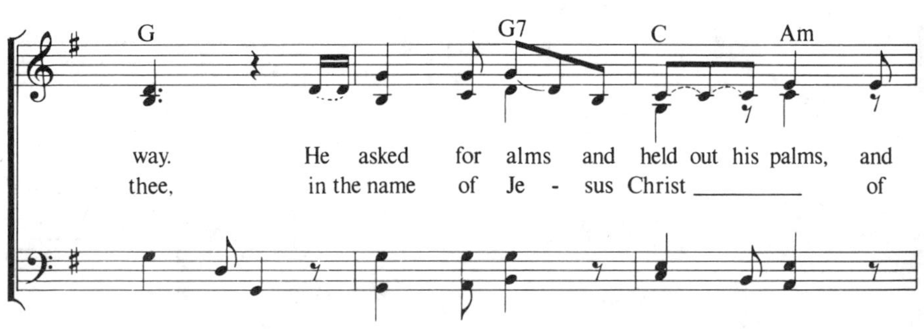
G
G7
C
Am
way. He asked for alms and held out his palms, and
thee, in the name of Je - sus Christ of

D7
1. G
2. G
this is what Pe - ter did say:
Naz - a-reth, rise up and walk!' He went

D7
walk - ing and leap - ing and prais - ing God,
G
walk - ing and leap - ing and prais - ing God. 'In the
C
Am
name of Je - sus Christ of
D7
G
Naz - a-reth, rise up and walk.'

51. There is a balm in Gilead

Capo 1 (E)

North American spiritual
Arr. Betty Pulkingham

Easily, not fast
Refrain
F(E)
There is a balm in Gil - e - ad to make the wounded
C7(B7)
F(E)
whole. There is a balm in Gil - e - ad to
B♭M7(AM7) C7(B7) F(E) Fine
Verses
F(E)
heal the sin - sick soul.
1. Some - times I feel dis -
2. If you can - not sing like
Gm(F♯m) F(E) C7(B7) F(E)
couraged, and think my work's in vain, but then the Ho - ly
an - gels, if you can - not preach like Paul, you can tell the love of
Gm(F♯m) B♭M7(AM7) C7(B7) F(E) B♭(A) C7(B7)
Spi - rit re - vives my soul a - gain. There is a
Je - sus and say he died for all.

52. Dear Lord and Father

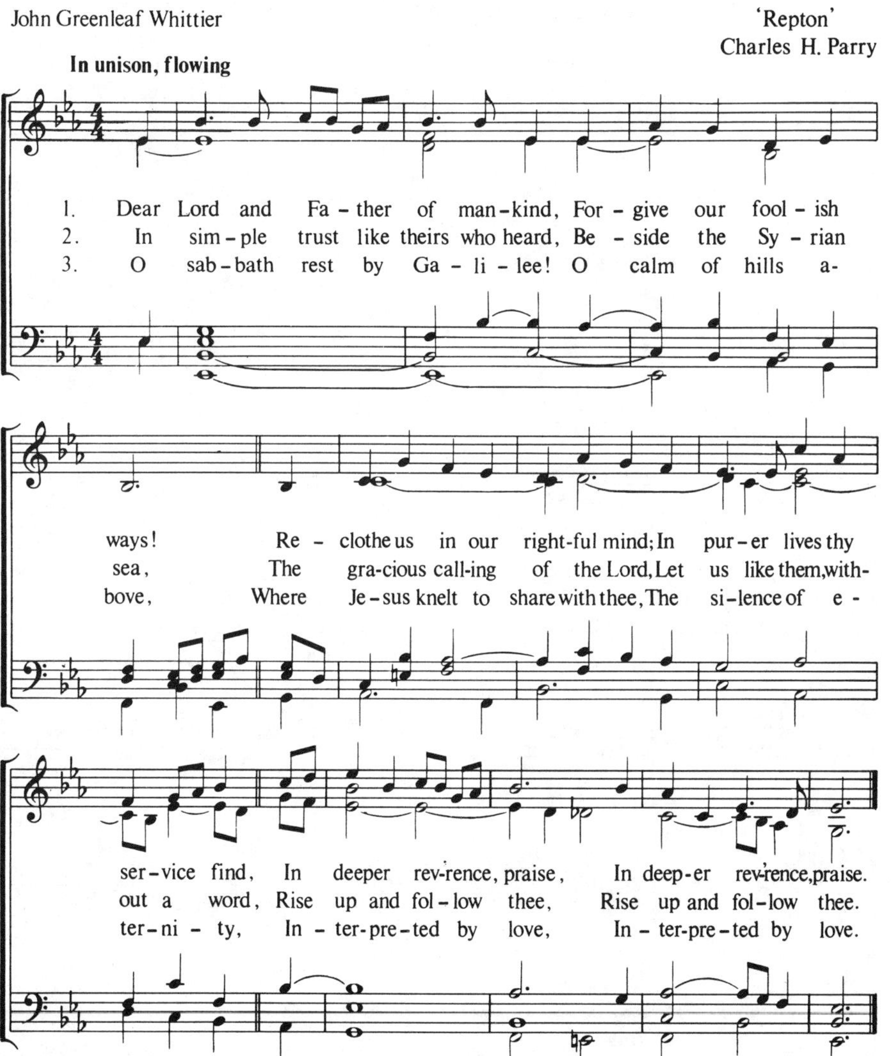
John Greenleaf Whittier
'Repton'
Charles H. Parry
In unison, flowing
1. Dear Lord and Fa - ther of man - kind, For - give our fool - ish
2. In sim - ple trust like theirs who heard, Be - side the Sy - rian
3. O sab - bath rest by Ga - li - lee! O calm of hills a-
ways! Re - clothe us in our right-ful mind; In pur - er lives thy
sea, The gra-cious call-ing of the Lord, Let us like them, with-
bove, Where Je - sus knelt to share with thee, The si - lence of e -
ser - vice find, In deeper rev-rence, praise, In deep-er rev-rence, praise.
out a word, Rise up and fol - low thee, Rise up and fol - low thee.
ter - ni - ty, In - ter - pre - ted by love, In - ter - pre - ted by love.

4. With that deep hush subduing all
Our words and works that drown
The tender whisper of thy call,
As noiseless let thy blessing fall
As fell thy manna down.

5. Drop thy still dews of quietness
Till all our strivings cease:
Take from our souls the strain and stress,
And let our ordered lives confess
The beauty of thy peace.

6. Breathe through the heats of our desire
Thy coolness and thy balm;
Let sense be dumb — let flesh retire;
Speak through the earthquake, wind, and fire,
O still small voice of calm!

53. The bell song*

Symphony of Souls
Arr. Betty Pulkingham

With quiet joy
E
1. You got-ta have love in your heart. You got-ta have love in your heart. You knew it was
peace on your mind. You got-ta have peace on your mind. You knew it was
joy in your soul. You got-ta have joy in your soul. The love of
la la la la etc.

* The Trees Group conceived this song as a delicate expression of praise through the use of bells and other small percussion instruments. Even a set of keys or a few coins from your pocket can be 'jingled' to add to the happy sound.

Suggested strum for guitar: the following rhythm with open strings sounding at ▼

A
E
Je - sus right from the start.
Je - sus there all the time.
Je - sus will make you whole.
D
A
You got-ta have love in your heart.
You got-ta have peace on your mind.
You got-ta have joy in your soul.
E
1.-4.
5.
2. You got-ta have
3. You got-ta have
4. La la la la
You got-ta know
D
A
E
(repeat ad lib.)
Fine
Je - - - sus in your heart.

54. By your stripes

Based on Isaiah 53: 5

Pamela Greenwood
Arr. Jeanne Harper

Boldly
C
F
By your stripes, Lord, I'm healed, hal - le - lu jah! In your
G7
C
word it is re-vealed, hal - le - lu - yah! Yes, you
F
bore it all for me on the cross of Cal - va - ry so that
G
C
now I can go free, hal - le - lu - jah!

Songs of the Kingdom . . .
The Body of Christ

55. Alleluia! sing to Jesus

William Dix

'Hyfrydol'
Rowland Prichard
Descant by Betty Pulkingham

With dignity

Descant
5. Al - le - lu - ia! Sing to Je - sus! His the scep - ter,
1. Al - le - lu - ia! sing to Je - sus! His the scep - ter,
2. Al - le - lu - ia! not as or - phans Are we left in
3. Al - le - lu - ia! bread of hea - ven, Thou on earth our

his the throne, al - le - lu - ia! Al - le - lu - ia! His the
his the throne; Al - le - lu - ia! his the tri - umph,
sor - row now; Al - le - lu - ia! he is near us,
food, our stay! Al - le - lu - ia! here the sin - ful

vic - to - ry, the vic - t'ry a - lone. Al - le - lu - ia! Al - le - lu -
His the vic - to - ry a - lone; Hark! the songs of peace - ful
Faith be - lieves, nor ques-tions how: Though the cloud from sight re -
Flee to thee from day to day: In - ter - ces - sor, friend of
ia! Al - le - lu - ia! Al-le - lu - ia! Al - le -
Zi - on Thun - der like a migh - ty flood; Je - sus
ceived him, When the for - ty days were o'er, Shall our
sin - ners, Earth's re - deem - er, plead for me, Where the
lu - ia! Al - - le - lu - ia! Al - le - lu - - ia!
out of ev - 'ry na - tion Hath re - deemed us by his blood.
hearts for - get his prom - ise, 'I am with you ev - er more?'
songs of all the sin - less Sweep a - cross the crys - tal sea.

4. Alleluia! king eternal,
   Thee the Lord of lords we own:
   Alleluia! born of Mary,
   Earth thy footstool, heav'n thy throne:
   Thou within the veil hast entered,
   Robed in flesh, our great high priest:
   Thou on earth both priest and victim
   In the eucharistic feast.

5. Alleluia! sing to Jesus!
   His the scepter, his the throne;
   Alleluia! his the triumph,
   His the victory alone;
   Hark! the songs of holy Zion
   Thunder like a mighty flood;
   Jesus out of every nation
   Hath redeemed us by his blood.

56. Blow, thou cleansing wind

Alan Teage

'Hyfrydol'
Rowland Prichard

1. Blow, thou cleansing wind from heaven,
   Burn, thou fire, within our hearts.
   Spirit of the Lord, possess us,
   Fill our lives in every part.
   Mind of Christ, be thou our ruler,
   Word of truth, be thou our guide;
   Leave no part of us unhallowed.
   Come, O come in us abide.

2. Fill thy church, inspire and strengthen,
   Chasten, mould, empower and lead.
   Make us one, and make us joyful,
   Give us grace for every need.
   Be our life, build firm thy kingdom.
   Be our strength, who are but frail.
   Then indeed against us never
   Shall the gates of hell prevail.

3. Win the world! Baptize the nations!
   Open every blinded eye.
   Leave no sinner unconvicted;
   Leave no soul untouched and dry.
   Conquering love, take thou the kingdom,
   Rule thou over all our days;
   Then in glory and rejoicing
   Earth shall echo with thy praise.

57. Jesus

Debby Kerner
Arr. Betty Pulkingham

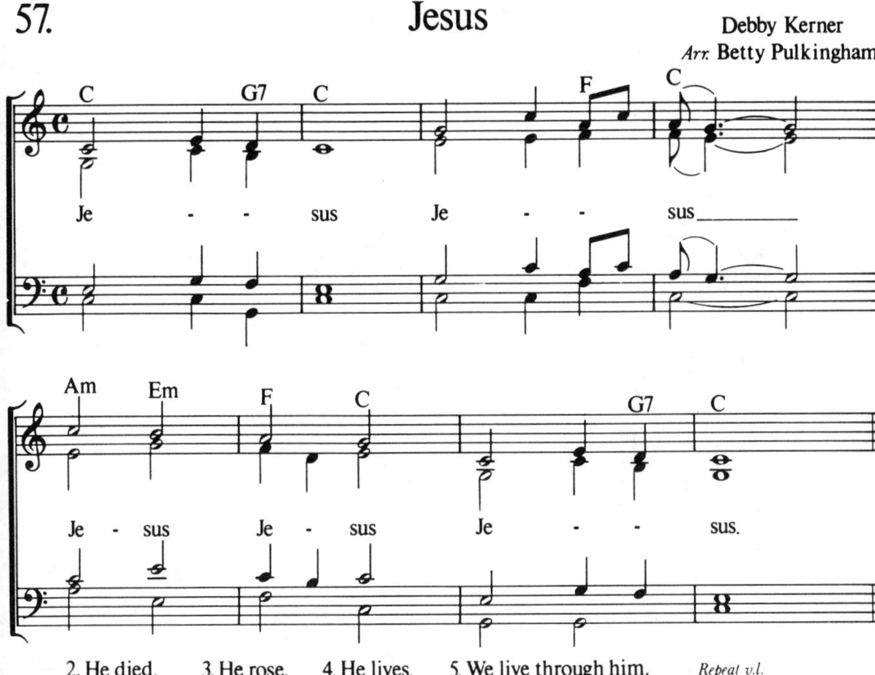
C
G7
C
F
C
Je - - sus Je - - sus
Am
Em
F
C
G7
C
Je - sus Je - sus Je - - sus.

2. He died. 3. He rose. 4. He lives. 5. We live through him. *Repeat v.l.*

58. Seek ye first

(2-part round)

Karen Lafferty

1
D
F♯m
G
D
G
D
A sus 4-3
Seek ye first the King-dom of God, and his righteous - ness,
and all these things shall be add-ed un-to you; al - le - lu, al - le
A7
2
Asus 4 - 3
lu - ia. Al - le - lu - ia, al - le - lu - ia,
al - le - lu - ia, al - le - lu, al-le - lu - ia.

59. Fear not! rejoice and be glad

Adapted from Joel 2,3,4.

Priscilla Wright

With breadth
Refrain
Em
Fear not, re - joice and be glad, the

B7
Em
Lord hath done a great thing; hath poured out his Spi - rit on

Em
B7
Em
Fine
Verses
all man - kind, on those who con - fess his name.
1. The
2. Ye
3. My
4. My

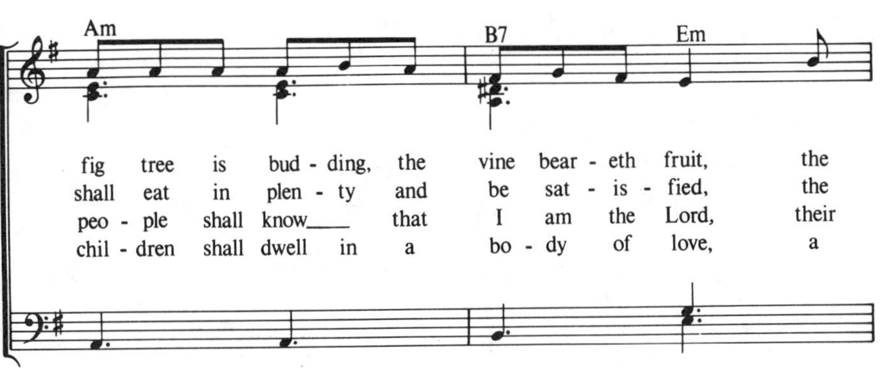
Am
B7
Em
fig tree is bud - ding, the vine bear - eth fruit, the
shall eat in plen - ty and be sat - is - fied, the
peo - ple shall know___ that I am the Lord, their
chil - dren shall dwell in a bo - dy of love, a

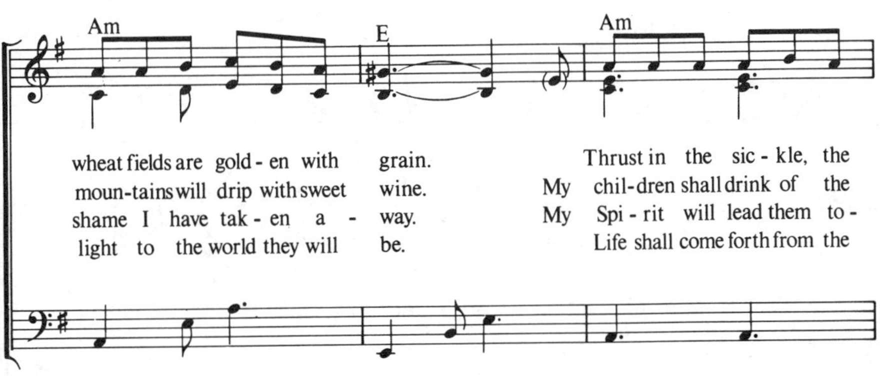
Am
E
Am
wheat fields are gold - en with grain. Thrust in the sic - kle, the
moun-tains will drip with sweet wine. My chil-dren shall drink of the
shame I have tak - en a - way. My Spi - rit will lead them to -
light to the world they will be. Life shall come forth from the

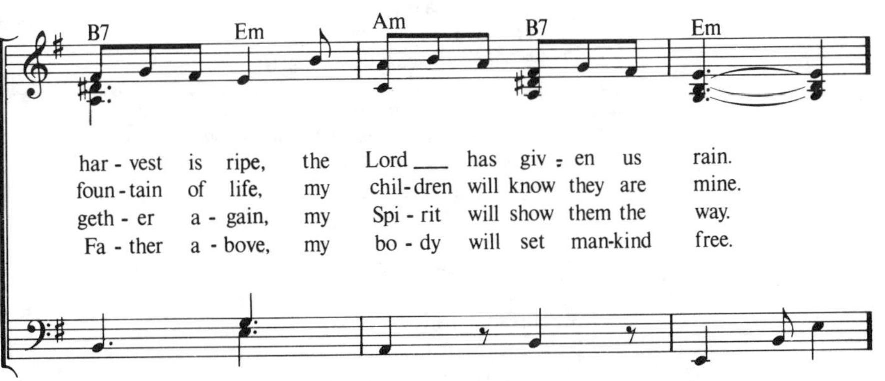
B7
Em
Am
B7
Em
har - vest is ripe, the Lord___ has giv - en us rain.
foun - tain of life, my chil-dren will know they are mine.
geth - er a - gain, my Spi - rit will show them the way.
Fa - ther a - bove, my bo - dy will set man-kind free.

60. God is building a house

Verses 2,3,4 – Hong Sit

Anon.
Arr. Betty Pulkingham

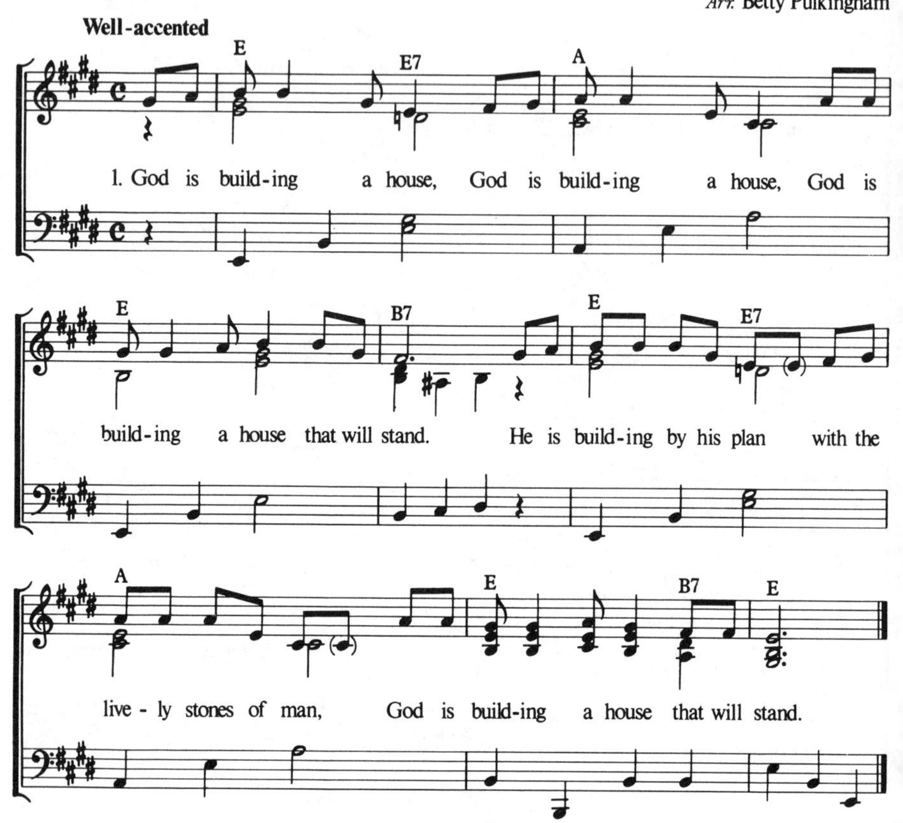
Well-accented
E
E7
A
1. God is build-ing a house, God is build-ing a house, God is
E
B7
E
E7
build-ing a house that will stand. He is build-ing by his plan with the
A
E
B7
E
live - ly stones of man, God is build-ing a house that will stand.

2. God is building a house, *(repeat)*
   God is building a house that will stand.
   With apostles, prophets, pastors,
   With evangelists and teachers,
   God is building a house that will stand.

3. Christ is head of this house, *(repeat)*
   Christ is head of this house that will stand.
   He abideth in its praise,
   Will perfect it in its ways,
   Christ is head of this house that will stand.

4. We are part of this house, *(repeat)*
   We are part of this house that will stand.
   We are called from ev'ry nation
   To enjoy his full salvation,
   We are part of this house that will stand.

61. The kingdom of God

Brian Howard
Bright and cheerful, not too fast
A D A D A E A A
1. The king - dom of God is neith - er lo here, nor
4. The Spir - it of God was not lost af - ter
5. The Prince of Peace has not gone a - way, He won't
6. The joy of the Lord is like a sing - ing lark, deep with-
lo there, no, the king - dom is a-
Pente - cost, no, the Spir - it is a-
let you stray, no, the Prince of Peace is a-
in your heart, let it flow so free - ly a-
1 2
mong us. The mong us.

2. The vict'ry of God is neither lo here, nor lo there,
No, the vict'ry is among us.

3. The power of God is neither lo here, nor lo there,
No, the power is among us.

63. I am the bread of life

Capo 3 (G)

S. Suzanne Toolan
Arr. Betty Pulkingham

Rich and full

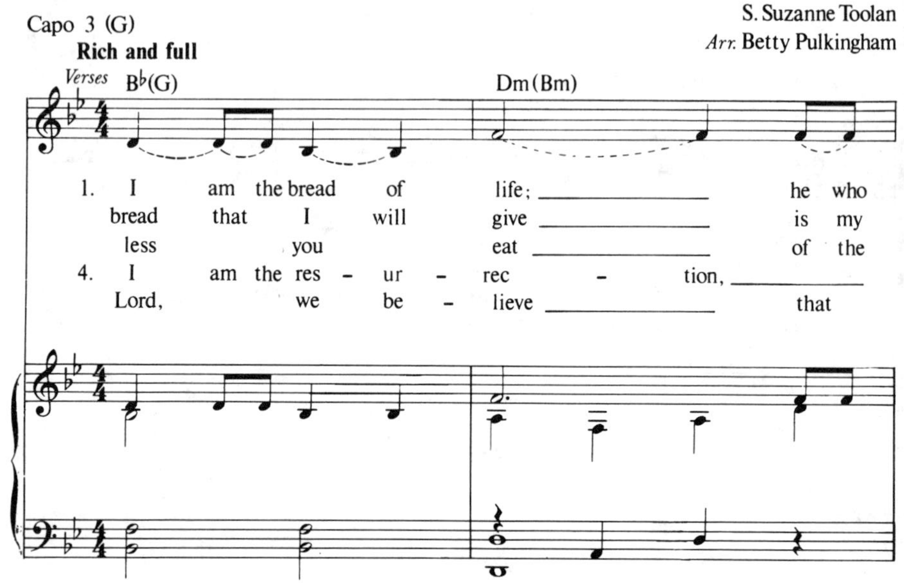

Verses B♭(G)
Dm(Bm)
1. I am the bread of life; he who
bread that I will give is my
less you eat of the
4. I am the res - ur - rec - tion,
Lord, we be - lieve that

E♭(C)
F(D)
comes to me shall not hun - ger; he who be-
flesh for the life of the world and he who
flesh of the Son of man and
I am the life. He who be-
you are the Christ, the

Song number 62 has been deleted from this edition inasmuch as the copyright holder has declined to grant the publishers permission for its continued use.

B♭(G) Dm(Bm) E♭(C) B♭(G)
lieves in me shall not thirst. No one can come to
eats of this bread, he shall live for-
drink of his blood, and drink of his
lieves in me, ev - en if he,
Son of God who has
E♭(C) Cm(Am) F(D)
Refrain
me un - less the Fa - ther draw him.
ev - er, he shall live for ev - er.
blood you shall not have life with - in you.
die, he shall live for - ev - er.
come in - to the world.
And I will
B♭(G) F(D) B♭(G) E♭(C)
raise him up, and I will raise him

F(D)
B♭(G)
E♭(C)
up, and I will raise him up on the
B♭(G)
F(D)
1-4
B♭(G)
B♭(G) final ending
last day.
2. The
3. Un -
5. Yes,
day.
64.
Oh, the blood of Jesus
Anon.
Arr. Betty Pulkingham
Capo 1 (E)
Quietly
F(E)
B♭(A)
F(E)
C7(B7)
F(E)
1. Oh, the blood of Je - sus, oh, the blood of Je - sus,
2. Oh, the word of Je - sus, oh, the word of Je - sus,
3. Oh, the love of Je - sus, oh, the love of Je - sus,

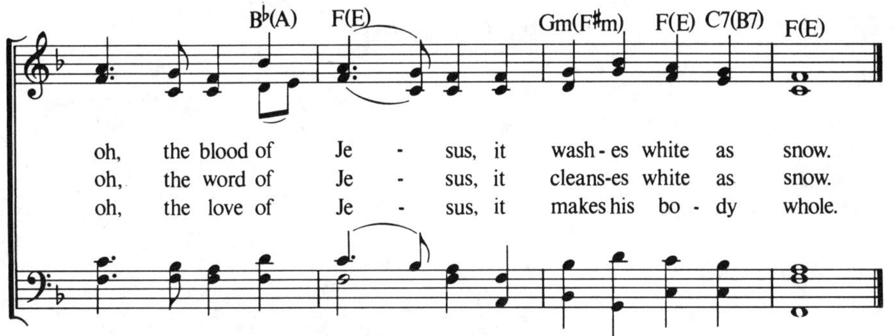
B♭(A) F(E) Gm(F♯m) F(E) C7(B7) F(E)
oh, the blood of Je - sus, it wash - es white as snow.
oh, the word of Je - sus, it cleans-es white as snow.
oh, the love of Je - sus, it makes his bo - dy whole.

'Oh, the blood of Jesus' may be sung in sequence with the following:

65. At the cross

Capo 1 (E)

Sankey
Arr. Betty Pulkingham

Smoothly

F(E) C7(B7)
At the cross, at the cross where I first saw the light, And the

F(E) F7(E7) B♭(A)
bur-den of my heart rolled a - way, It was there by faith I re-

F(E) C7(B7) F(E) B♭(A) F(E)
ceived my sight, And now I am hap - py all the day.

66. A new commandment

John 13: 34 - 35

Anon.
Arr. Betty Pulkingham

Warmly
D
Bm
Em7
A new com - mand-ment I give un - to
A7
D
Bm
Em7
you, that you love one an - oth - er as I have loved
A7
F♯m
Bm
Em
A7
you, that you love one an - oth - er as I have loved
D
D7
G
A7
D
A
you. By this shall all men know you are my dis-

Bm
G
A
Bm
3
G
D
ci - ples if you have love one to an - oth - er.

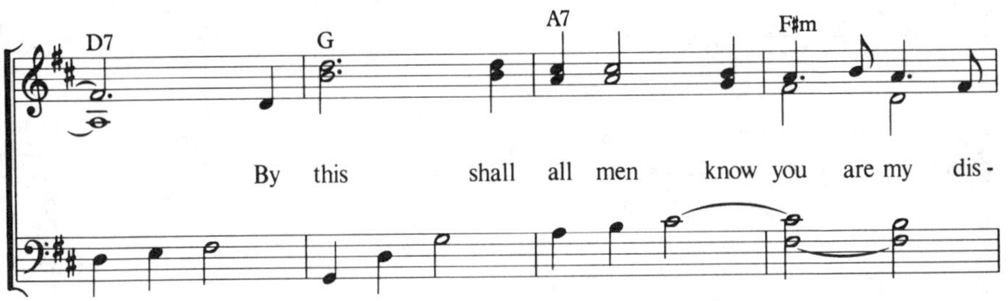
D7
G
A7
F♯m
By this shall all men know you are my dis -

Bm
Em
A
Bm
3
G
D
ci - ples if you have love one to an - oth - er.
3

67. God and man at table are sat down

Robert Stamps
Arr. Jeanne Harper

With dignity and gentleness
Em
Bm7
Em
D
A7
D
B7
Em
B7
Em
Am7
Bm7
1. Em
2. Em
1. Oh wel-come, all ye no - ble saints of old As
2. El - ders, mar - tyrs, all are fall - ing down,
3. Who is this who spreads the vic - t'ry feast?
now be - fore your ve - ry eyes un - fold The
Pro-phets, pa - tri - archs are gath - 'ring round. What
Who is this who makes our war - ring cease?
won - ders all so long a - go fore - told:
an - gels longed to see now man has found.
Je - sus, ri - sen Sa - viour, Prince of Peace.
God and man at ta - ble are sat down. down.

68.

Glory be to Jesus

'Caswall'

Tr. Edward Caswall — Friedrick Filitz

Descant Betty Pulkingham

With breadth

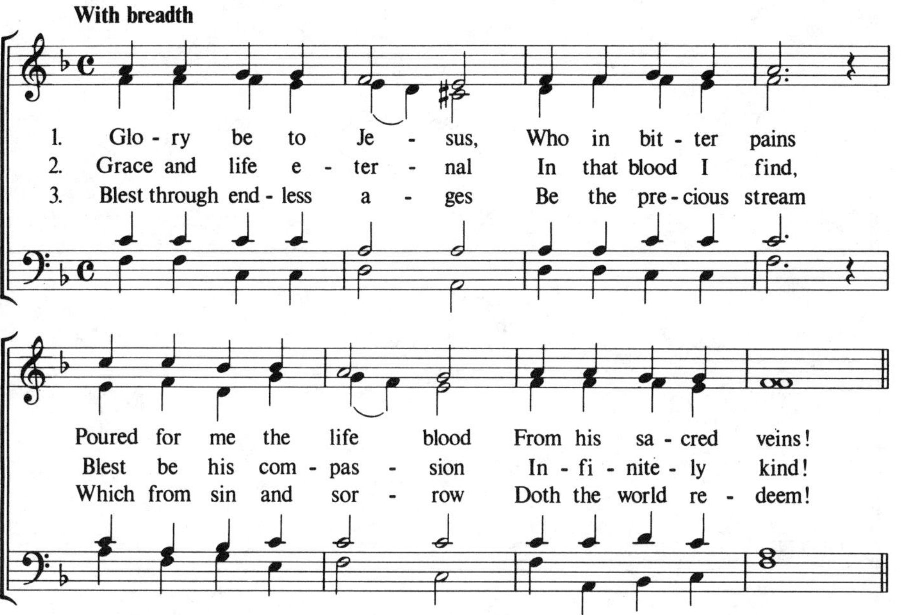

1. Glo - ry be to Je - sus, Who in bit - ter pains
2. Grace and life e - ter - nal In that blood I find,
3. Blest through end - less a - ges Be the pre - cious stream
Poured for me the life blood From his sa - cred veins!
Blest be his com - pas - sion In - fi - nite - ly kind!
Which from sin and sor - row Doth the world re - deem!

4. Oft as earth exulting
Wafts its praise on high,
Angel hosts, rejoicing,
Make their glad reply.

5. Lift ye then your voices;
Swell the mighty flood;
Louder still and louder
Praise the precious blood.

Optional descant last stanza

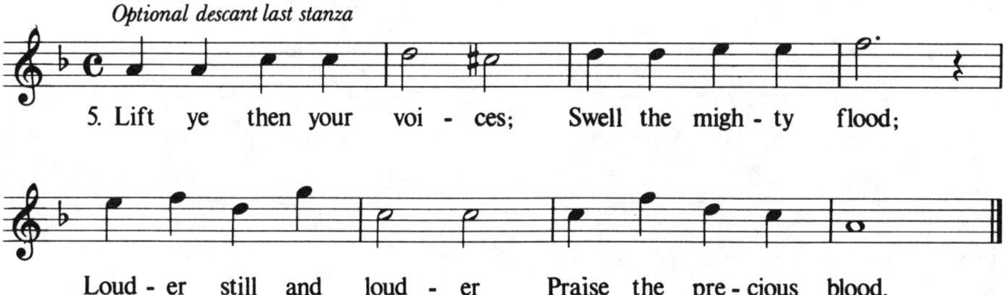

5. Lift ye then your voi - ces; Swell the migh - ty flood;
Loud - er still and loud - er Praise the pre - cious blood.

69. We really want to thank you, Lord

Capo 2(C)

Ed Baggett
Arr. Betty Pulkingham

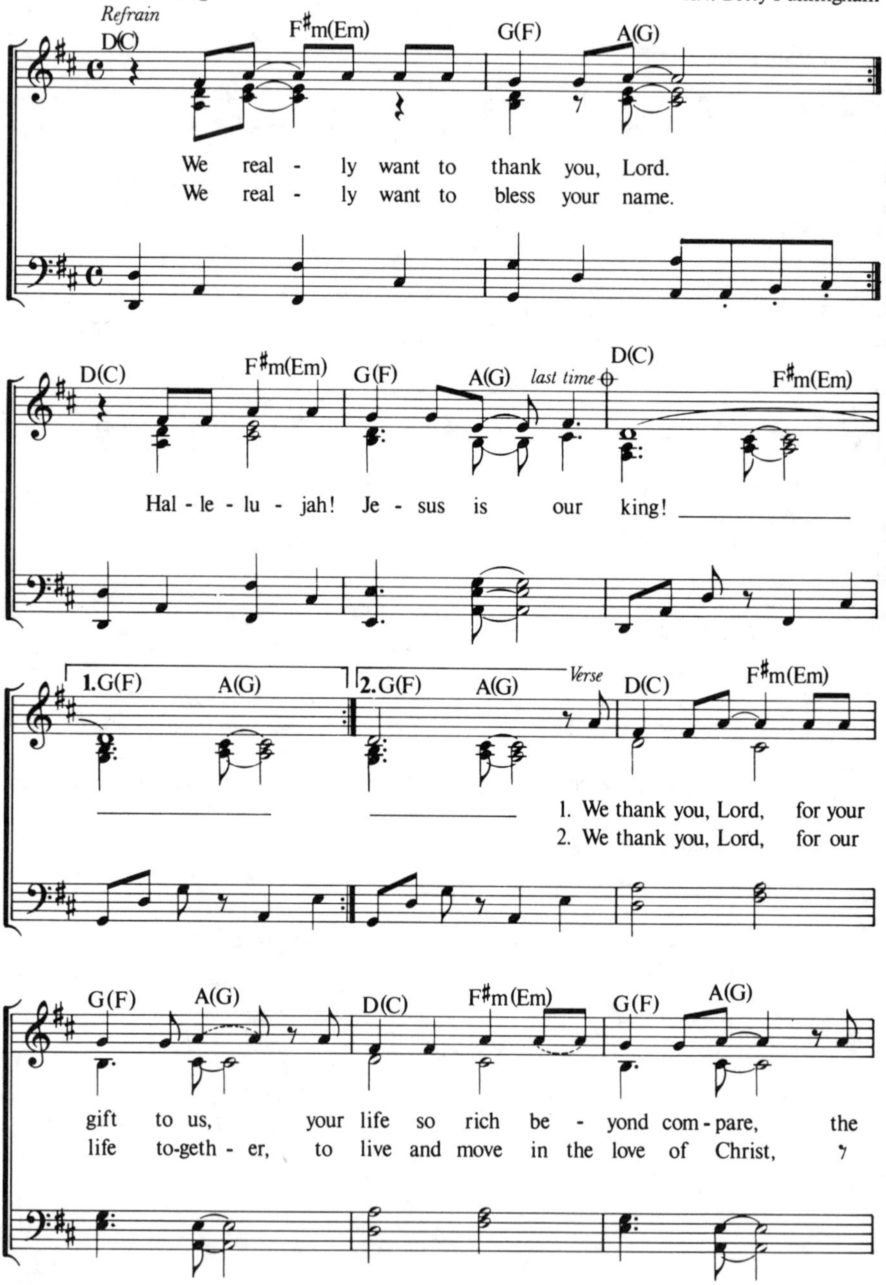

With a swing

Refrain

We really want to thank you, Lord.
We really want to bless your name.
Hallelujah! Jesus is our king! ______

1.G(F) A(G) ______ 2.G(F) A(G) ______

Verse

1. We thank you, Lord, for your gift to us, your life so rich beyond compare, the
2. We thank you, Lord, for our life together, to live and move in the love of Christ,

D(C) F♯m (Em) G(F) A(G)
gift of your bo - dy here on earth of
ten - der - ness which sets us free to
D(C) G(F) A(G)
Refrain
which we sing and share.
serve you with our lives.
D(C) G(F) D(C)
king!

70. This is my commandment

John 15: 11-12

Anon
Arr. Betty Pulkingham

Simply
E
This is my command-ment that you love one an-oth - er, that your
B7
1 E
Fine
2 E
joy may be full.
full; that your
A
E
joy may be full, that your
A
E
D.C. al Fine
joy may be full,

Other verses may be added:
eg. This is my commandment that you 'trust one another...'
'serve one another...'
'lay down your lives...'

71. The king of love

H.W. Baker
Based on Psalm 23

'St. Columba'
Traditional Irish melody

In flowing style

D D A D A7 Bm7 F#m G 3 A (Em)
1. The king of love my shep-herd is, Whose good-ness fail - eth nev -
2. Where streams of liv - ing wa - ter flow, My ransomed soul he lead -
3. Per - verse and fool - ish oft I strayed, But yet in love he sought

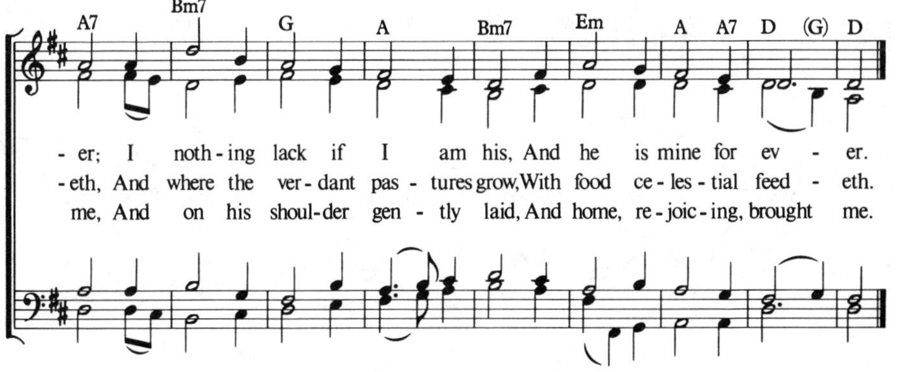

A7 Bm7 G A Bm7 Em A A7 D (G) D
- er; I noth - ing lack if I am his, And he is mine for ev - er.
- eth, And where the ver - dant pas - tures grow, With food ce - les - tial feed - eth.
me, And on his shoul-der gen - tly laid, And home, re - joic - ing, brought me.

4. In death's dark vale I fear no ill
   With thee, dear Lord, beside me;
   Thy rod and staff my comfort still,
   Thy cross before to guide me.

5. Thou spread'st a table in my sight;
   Thy unction grace bestoweth;
   And o what transport of delight
   From thy pure chalice floweth!

6. And so through all the length of days
   Thy goodness faileth never:
   Good shepherd, may I sing thy praise
   Within thy house for ever.

*Guitar chords and 4-part harmonization not designed to be used together.

72. Glorious things of thee are spoken

John Newton

'Abbot's Leigh'
Cyril Taylor

Majestic

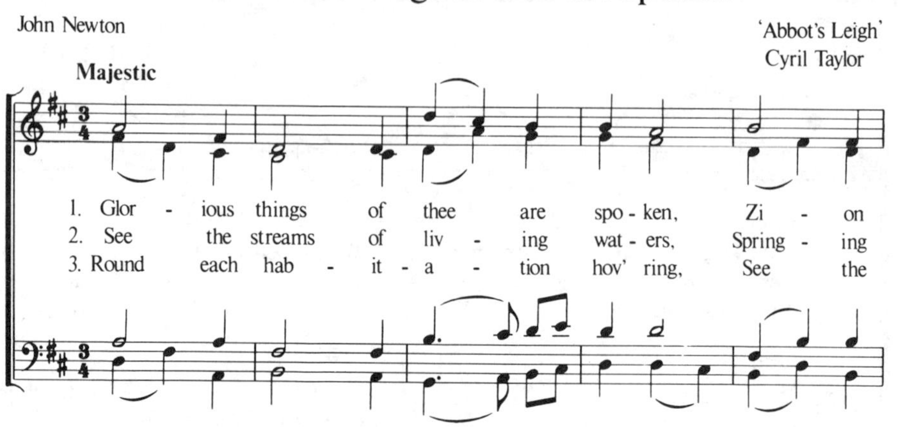
1. Glor - ious things of thee are spo - ken, Zi - on
2. See the streams of liv - ing wat - ers, Spring - ing
3. Round each hab - it - a - tion hov' ring, See the

ci - ty of our God. He whose word can -
from e - ter - nal love, Well sup - ply thy
cloud and fire ap - pear! For a glo - ry

not be bro - ken, Formed thee for his own a - bode:
sons and daugh-ters, And all fear of want re - move:
and a cov'- ring Show - ing that the Lord is near:

On the rock of ag - es found - ed, What can
Who can faint while such a riv - er Ev - er
He who gives them dai - ly man - na, He who
shake thy sure re - pose? With sal - va - tion's
flows their thirst to assuage? Grace which like the
list - ens when they cry: Let him hear the
walls sur - round - ed, Thou may'st smile at all thy foes.
Lord, the giv - er, Ev - er flows from age to age.
loud hos - an - na, Ri - sing to his throne on high.

4. Saviour since of Zion's city
   I through grace a member am,
Let the world deride or pity,
   I will glory in thy name;

Fading is the worldling's pleasure,
   All his boasted pomp and show;
Solid joys and lasting treasure
   None but Zion's children know.

5. Blest inhabitants of Zion;
   Washed in the Redeemer's blood!
Jesus, whom their souls rely on,
   Makes them kings and priests to God.

'Tis his love his people raises
   Over self to reign as kings:
And as priests, his solemn praises
   Each for a thank-off'ring brings.

72. Glorious things of thee are spoken

'Austria'
Franz Joseph Haydn

Majestic

Suffer–Reign . . .
Songs of Faith and Victory

74. God has called you

Diane Davis

C
F
C
1. God has called (name), he will not fail ______ (him, her).
2. God has called you, he will not fail ______ you.
3. God has called us, we will not fail ______ him.

G
G7
C
God has called (name), he will not fail ______ (him, her).
God has called you, he will not fail ______ you.
God has called us, we will not fail ______ him.

F
C
God has called (name), he will not fail ______ (him, her), so
God has called you, he will not fail ______ you, so
God has called us, we will not fail ______ him, so

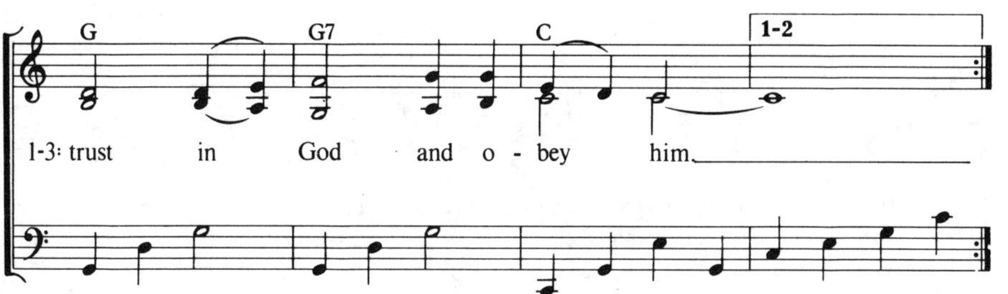
G
G7
C
1-2
1-3: trust in God and o - bey him.

final ending
G
G7
C
So trust in God and o - bey him.

75. How firm a foundation

John Rippon

'Lyons'
Based on Michael Haydn

With energy
1. How firm a foun-da-tion, ye saints of the Lord, is laid for your faith in his ex-cel-lent word! What more can he say than to you he hath said, To you that for ref-uge to Je-sus have fled?
2. 'Fear not, I am with thee; O be not dis-mayed! For I am thy God, and will still give thee aid; I'll strength-en thee, help thee, and cause thee to stand, Up-held by my right-eous, om-ni-po-tent hand.
3. 'When through the deep wa-ters I call thee to go, The riv-ers of woe shall not thee o-ver-flow; For I will be with thee, thy trou-bles to bless, And sanc-ti-fy to thee thy deep-est dis-tress.

4. 'When through fiery trials thy pathway shall lie,
My grace, all-sufficient, shall be thy supply;
The flame shall not hurt thee; I only design
Thy dross to consume, and thy gold to refine.

5. 'The soul that to Jesus has fled for repose,
I will not, I will not desert to his foes;
That soul, though all hell shall endeavor to shake,
I'll never, no, never, no, never forsake.'

75. How firm a foundation

Anne Steele
Arr. Betty Pulkingham

With sweeping breadth

D7
G
C
G
C
G
C

D
D7
C
Am7
Bm7
Em
CM7
D

G
Bm7
Em
G

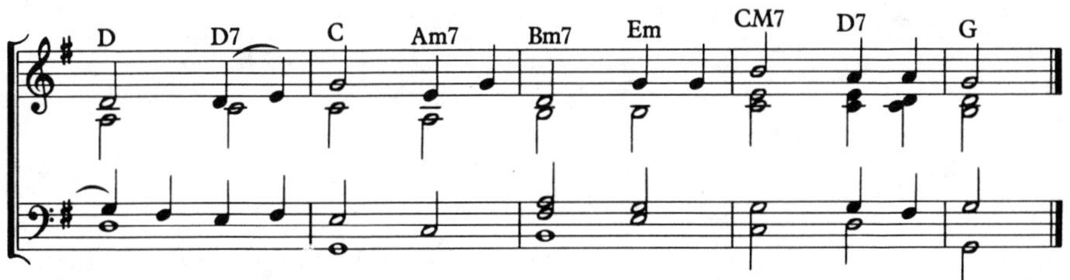
D
D7
C
Am7
Bm7
Em
CM7
D7
G

76. Complete in him

Anon.
Arr. Betty Pulkingham

Well accented
Verses
D
A
D
D7
G
D
A7
D
1. The full-ness of the God-head bod-i-ly dwell-eth in my Lord. The full-ness of the God-head bod-i-ly dwell-eth in my Lord. The full-ness of the God-head bod-i-ly dwell-eth in my Lord, and
2. It's not by works of righteous-ness, but by his grace a-lone It's not by works of righteous-ness, but by his grace a-lone. It's not by works of righteous-ness, but by his grace a-lone, that
3. There's no-thing more that I can do, for Je-sus did it all. There's no-thing more that I can do, for Je-sus did it all. There's no-thing more that I can do, for Je-sus did it all, and
we are com-plete in him.

Refrain
D
G
D
Com - plete, com-plete, com-plete in him, we are com-
A
D
(Hal - le lu jah, we're)
plete in him. Com-plete, com - plete, com-
G
D
A7
D
plete in him, we are com-plete in him.

77. The Holy Ghost Medley

Capo 3 (A)

Arr. Betty Pulkingham

Well-accented rhythm
C(A) G(E) C(A)
Je - sus gave her wa - ter that was not from the well,
C(A) Am(F♯m) D7(B7) G(E)
Gave her liv - ing wa - ter and sent her forth to tell; She
C(A) F(D) C(A) C(A) F(D) C(A)
went a-way sing - ing, and came back bring - ing
F(D) C(A) G(E) Fine C(A) C7(A7)
oth - ers for the wa - ter that was not from the well.

F(D)
C7(A7)
F(D)
Drink - ing at the springs of liv - ing wa - ter,
C7(A7)
F(D)
Hap - py now am I, My soul is sat - is - fied,
C7(A7)
F(D)
Drink - ing at the springs of liv - ing wa - ter, What a
C7(A7)
F(D)
won - der - ful and boun - te - ous sup - ply. Spring up, O

F(D)
B♭(G)
F(D)
well, with - in my soul. Spring up, O
C(A)
well, and o - ver - flow; Spring up, O
F(D)
B♭(G)
F(D)
well, flow out through me. Spring up, O
C(A)
F(D)
well, set oth - ers free.

F(D) F7(D7) B♭(G) F(D)

There's a river of life flow-ing out through me, It
There's a foun-tain flowing from the Sav - iour's side,
There's a ris - en Saviour at the Fa - ther's throne,

G7(E7) C7(A7)

makes the lame to walk and the blind to see,
All my sins for - given in that pre - cious tide.
Ev - er in - ter - ceding for his ve - ry own,

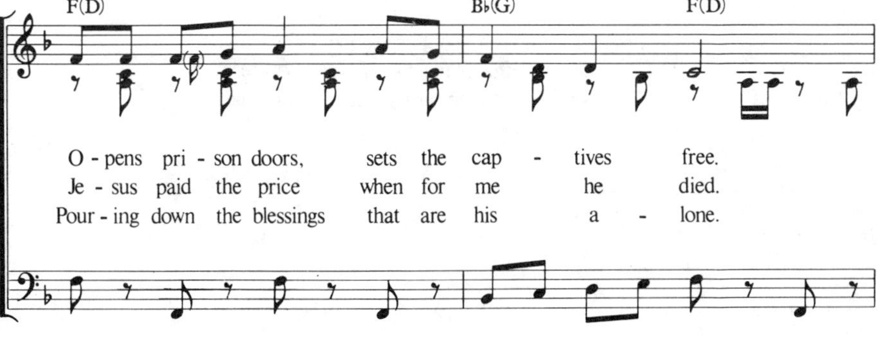
F(D)
B♭(G)
F(D)
O - pens pri - son doors, sets the cap - tives free.
Je - sus paid the price when for me he died.
Pour - ing down the blessings that are his a - lone.

F(D)
C7(A7)
There's a riv - er of life flow - ing out through
There's a foun - tain flow - ing from the Sa - viour's
There's a ris - en Sa - viour at the Fa - ther's
1-5
F(D)
6
F(D)
me.
side.
throne.
me.

4 There's a holy comforter who's sent from heaven,
All the glorious gifts are his, and have been given,
He'll/show us more of Jesus 'til the veil is riven.
There's a holy comforter who's sent from heaven.

5 There's a land of rest that we may enter now,
Freed from all our works and freed from Satan's power,
Just/resting in the Lord each moment and each hour.
There's a land of rest that we may enter now.

6 There's a full salvation wrought for you and me,
From/faith to faith and glory to glory e/ternally,
O/Lord, just take this life and let me live for thee.
There's a full salvation wrought for you and me.

Jesus gave her water – Anon.
Springs of living water – J.W. Peterson

Spring up, o well – Anon.
There's a river of life – L. Casebolt
Verses 2-6 – Betty Carr Pulkingham.

78. I have decided to follow Jesus

Paul Smith
Arr. Betty Pulkingham

With determination
C
1. I have de - cid - ed to fol - low Je - sus. I have de -
2. The world be - hind me, the cross be - fore me. The world be -
3. Tho' none go with me, still I will fol - low. Tho' none go
F
C
cid - ed to fol - low Je - sus. I have de - cid - ed to fol - low
hind me, the cross be - fore me. The world be - hind me, the cross be-
with me, still I will fol - low. Tho' none go with me, still I will
Am
C
G7
C
Je - sus,
fore me,
fol - low,
no turn - ing back, no turn - ing back.

4. Where Jesus leads me, I'll surely follow. *(repeat twice)*
   No turning back, no turning back.

5. Sing glory, glory and hallelujah. *(repeat twice)*
   No turning back, no turning back.

79. See the conqu'ror mounts in triumph

Christopher Wordsworth

'In Babilone'
Traditional Dutch melody

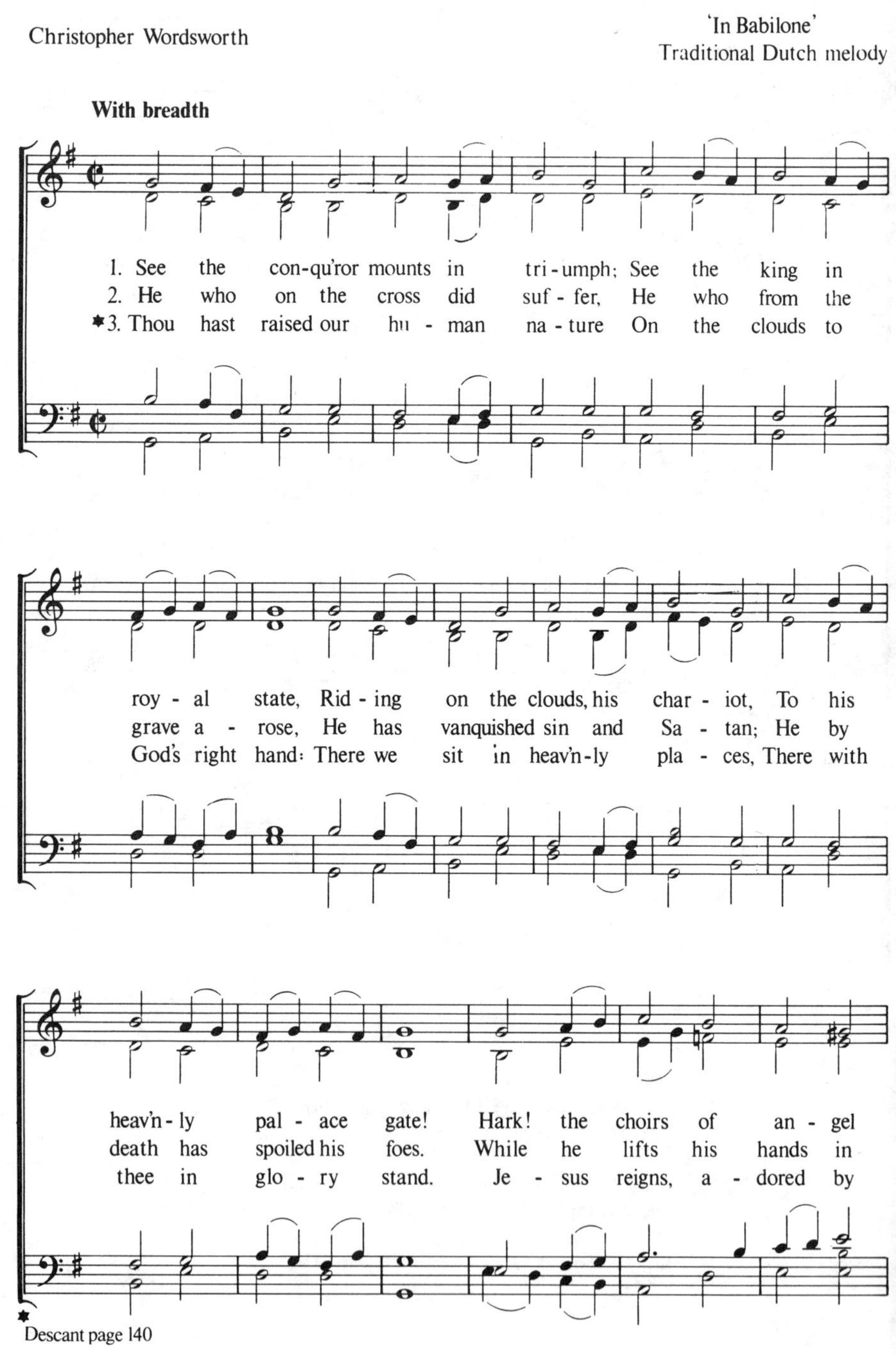

With breadth
1. See the con-qu'ror mounts in tri-umph; See the king in roy-al state, Rid-ing on the clouds, his char-iot, To his heav'n-ly pal-ace gate! Hark! the choirs of an-gel
2. He who on the cross did suf-fer, He who from the grave a-rose, He has vanquished sin and Sa-tan; He by death has spoiled his foes. While he lifts his hands in
*3. Thou hast raised our hu-man na-ture On the clouds to God's right hand: There we sit in heav'n-ly pla-ces, There with thee in glo-ry stand. Je-sus reigns, a-dored by

* Descant page 140

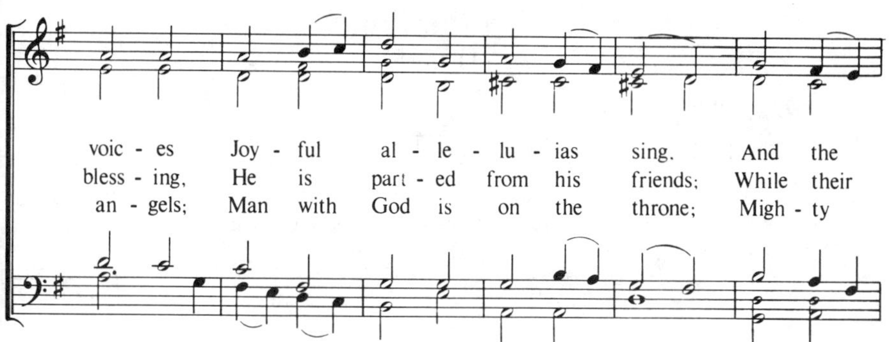
voic - es Joy - ful al - le - lu - ias sing. And the
bless - ing, He is part - ed from his friends; While their
an - gels; Man with God is on the throne; Migh - ty

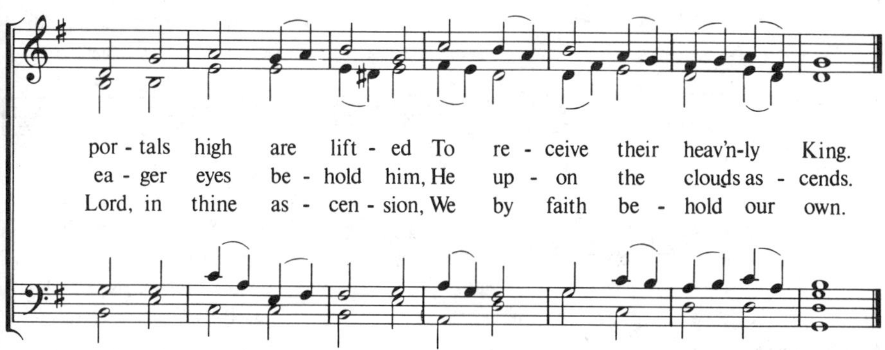
por - tals high are lift - ed To re - ceive their heav'n-ly King.
ea - ger eyes be - hold him, He up - on the clouds as - cends.
Lord, in thine as - cen - sion, We by faith be - hold our own.

80. Hail, thou once despised Jesus

John Blackwell
Martin Madan

'In Babilone'
Traditional Dutch melody

1. Hail, thou once despised Jesus!
Hail, thou Galilean King!
Thou didst suffer to release us;
Thou didst free salvation bring.
Hail, thou universal Saviour,
Bearer of our sin and shame.
By thy merit we find favour:
Life is given through thy name.

2. Paschal Lamb, by God appointed,
All our sins on thee were laid:
By almighty love anointed,
Thou hast full atonement made.
All thy people are forgiven
Through the virtue of thy blood:
Opened is the gate of heaven,
Peace is made 'twixt man and God.

3. Jesus, hail! enthroned in glory,
There for ever to abide;
All the heav'nly hosts adore thee,
Seated at thy Father's side.
There for sinners thou art pleading:
There thou dost our place prepare;
Ever for us interceding,
Till in glory we appear.

*4. Worship, honour, power, and blessing
Thou art worthy to receive:
Highest praises, without ceasing,
Meet it is for us to give.
Help, ye bright angelic spirits,
Bring your sweetest, noblest lays;
Help to sing our Saviour's merits,
Help to chant Emmanuel's praise!

'In Babilone'

(Descant)
Betty Pulkingham
With breadth
Descant
No.79
No.80
Melody
3. Thou hast raised our hu - man na - ture On the clouds to God's right hand. There we sit in heav'n - ly pla - ces, There with thee in glo - ry stand. Je - sus reigns adored by an - gels, Man with God is on the throne. Migh-ty Lord, in thine as - cen - sion, We by faith be - hold our own.
4. Wor - ship, hon-our, pow'r and bless-ing Thou art wor - thy to re - ceive. High - est prais - es with - out ceas - ing, Meet it is for us to give. Help ye bright an-gel - ic spi - rits, Bring your sweet - est no-blest lays. Help to sing our Sa - viour's mer - its, Help to chant Em - man - uel's praise.

81. He signed my deed

Anon.
Arr. Betty Pulkingham

Vigorous, well accented
E B7 E (A) E B7 E E B7 E (A)
He signed my deed with his a-ton-ing blood, He ev - er lives to
E B7 E E B7
make his prom - ise good. Though all the hosts of hell march in to
E B7 C#m(E) B7 E A E B7 E
make a sec-ond claim, They'll all march out at the men-tion of his name. They'll
[last time, like an echo]
E B7 E7 A E B7 E
all march out at the men - tion of His name.
Je - sus
(spoken last time)

82. Jesus is Lord

David J. Mansell

With majesty

1. Je - sus is Lord! Cre - a - tion's voice pro - claims it,
2. Je - sus is Lord! Yet from his throne e - ter - nal
3. Je - sus is Lord! O'er sin the migh - ty con - queror,

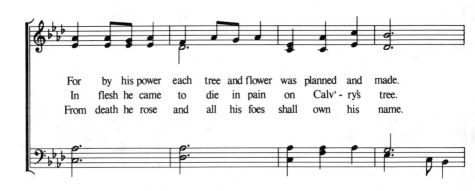

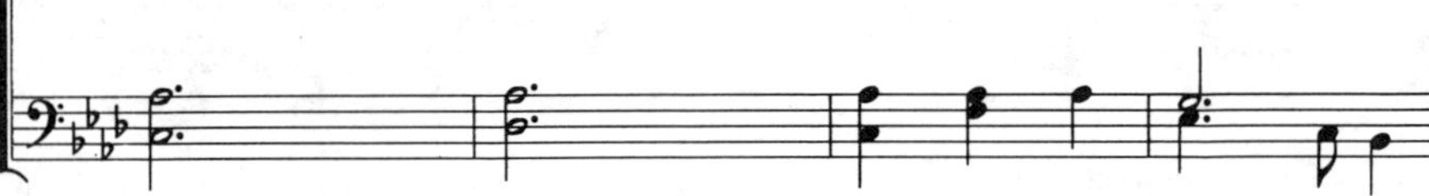

For by his power each tree and flower was planned and made.
In flesh he came to die in pain on Calv' - ry's tree.
From death he rose and all his foes shall own his name.

Je - sus is Lord! The u - ni - verse de - clares it.
Je - sus is Lord! From him all life pro - ceed - ing,
Je - sus is Lord! God sends his Ho - ly Spir - it

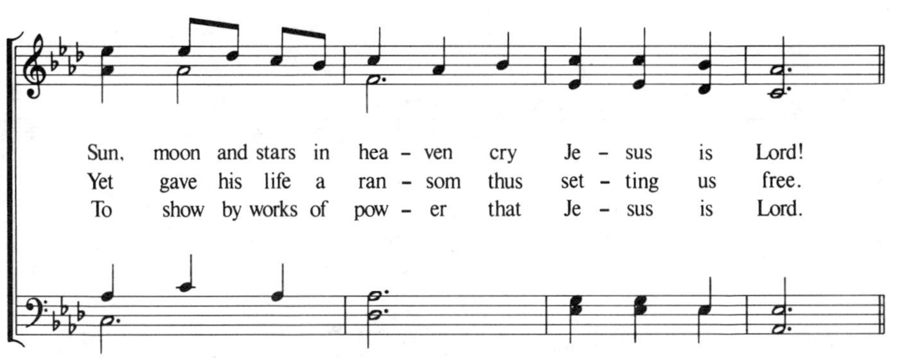
Sun, moon and stars in hea - ven cry Je - sus is Lord!
Yet gave his life a ran - som thus set - ting us free.
To show by works of pow - er that Je - sus is Lord.

Refrain
Je - sus is Lord! Je - sus is Lord!

Praise him with 'Hal - le - lu - jahs' for Je - sus is Lord!

83. The joy of the Lord

Anon.
Arr. Betty Pulkingham
Brightly
E
B7
1. The joy___ of the Lord ________ is my strength; the
2. If you___ want_ joy___ you must sing for it; if
3. The word of faith is nigh thee, ev - en in thy mouth; the
E
joy ___ of the Lord ___________ is my strength; the
you ___ want ___ joy ___ you must shout for it; if
word of faith is nigh thee, ev - en in thy mouth; the
A
joy ___ of the Lord ___________ is my strength; the
you ___ want _ joy ___ you must jump for it; the
word of faith is nigh thee, ev - en in thy mouth; the
E
B7
E
joy of the Lord is my strength.
joy of the Lord is my strength.
joy of the Lord is my strength.
A-

B7
- ha ha ha ha ha ha ha ha ha ha. A-
E
- ha ha ha ha ha ha ha ha ha ha. A-
A
- ha ha ha ha ha ha ha ha ha ha. The
E
B7
E
joy of the Lord is my strength.

84. I heard the Lord

Jacob Krieger
Arr. Betty Pulkingham

Capo 3(D)
With a delicate swing
F(D) B♭(G) F(D) B♭(G)
1. I heard the Lord call my name, li - sten close
love, love's his word, that's the mes-
love from a - bove set - tle on
Fa - ther all your days with the Son
F(D) C7(A7) F(D) C7(A7)
you'll hear the same. I heard the Lord call my name,
sage that I heard. His word is love, love's his word,
me like a dove. I felt his love from a - bove
and Spi - rit praise. And to the Fa - ther all your days
li - sten close you'll hear the same. I heard the
that's the mes - sage that I heard. His word is
set - tle on me like a dove. I felt his
with the Son and Spi - rit praise. And to the

F(D) B♭(G) F(D) B♭(G) F(D) C7(A7)
Lord call my name, li - sten close you'll hear the same.
love, love's his word, that's the mes - sage that I heard.
love from a - bove set - tle on me like a dove.
Fa - ther all your days with the Son and Spi - rit praise.
F(D) C7(A7) F(D)
1.-4. Take his hand, we are glo - ry bound.
1. Vs. 1, 3
2. Vs. 2, 4
Fine
A(F♯) Dm (Bm)
2. His word is
4. And to the
Place your hand in his and you will
G(E) G7(E7) C(A)
know, he will show you where to go.
3. I felt his
1. I heard the

85. And can it be?

Charles Wesley

'Sagina'
Thomas Campbell

Thoughtfully, not too slow

1. And can it be that I should gain An
2. 'Tis mys - t'ry all! th'im - mor - tal dies! Who
3. He left his fa - ther's throne a - bove, So

in - t'rest in the Sav - iour's blood?
can ex - plore his strange de - sign?
free, so in - fin - nite his grace;

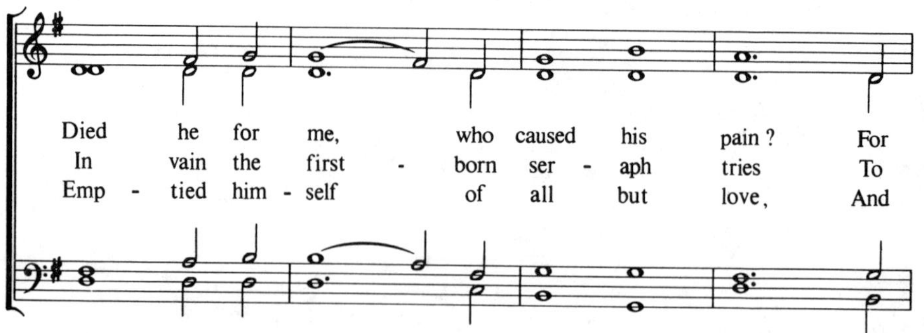
Died he for me, who caused his pain? For
In vain the first - born ser - aph tries To
Emp - tied him - self of all but love, And

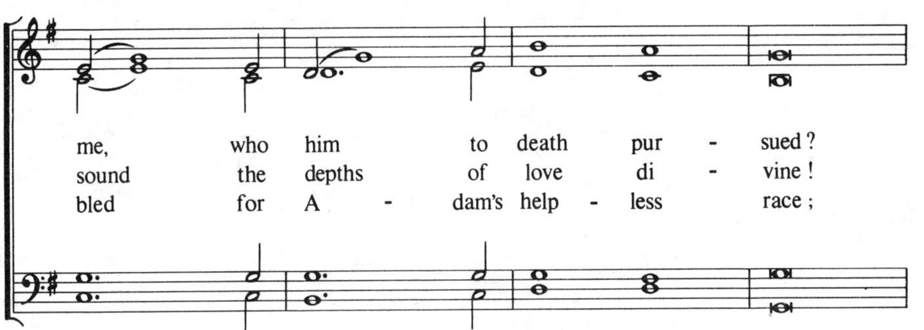
me, who him to death pur - sued?
sound the depths of love di - vine!
bled for A - dam's help - less race;

A - maz - ing love! how can it be That
'Tis mer - cy all! let earth a - dore, Let
'Tis mer - cy all, im - mense and free; For,

A–
thou, my God, shouldst die for me?
an - gel minds in - quire no more.
O my God, it found out me.

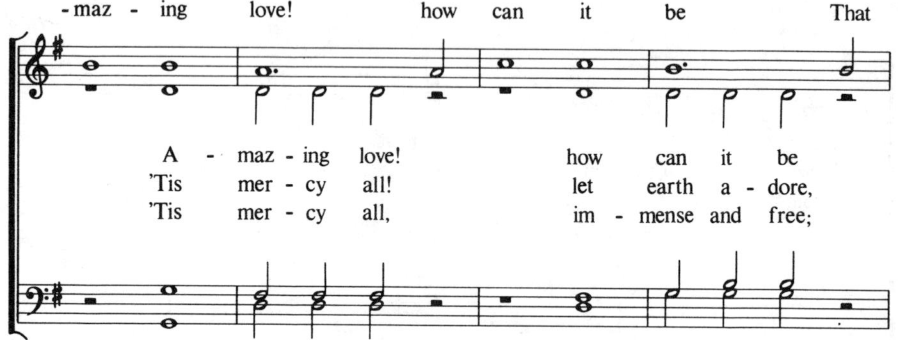

-maz - ing love! how can it be That
A - maz - ing love! how can it be
'Tis mer - cy all! let earth a - dore,
'Tis mer - cy all, im - mense and free;

thou, my God, shouldst die for me?
That thou my God, shouldst die for me?
Let an - gel minds in - quire no more.
For, O my God, it found out me.

4 Long my imprisoned spirit lay
Fast bound in sin and nature's night;
Thine eye diffused a quickening ray,
I woke, the dungeon flamed with light;
My chains fell off, my heart was free;
I rose, went forth, and followed thee.

5 No condemnation now I dread;
Jesus and all in him, is mine!
Alive in him, my living head,
And clothed in righteousness divine,
Bold I approach the eternal throne,
And claim the crown, through Christ my own.

Go Forth . . . Outreach

86. Alleluia! Sons of God, arise!

Mimi Farra

Triumphantly
Refrain
Al - le - lu - ia! Al - le - lu - ia! Al - le - lu - ia, sons of God, a - rise.
Al - le - lu - ia! Al - le - lu - ia!
sons of God, a - rise and fol - low the Lord.
Fine
Verses
1. Come and be clothed in his right - eous - ness; Come join the band who are called by his name.
2. Look at the world which is bound by sin; Walk in - to the midst of it pro - claim - ing my life.
V. 1. only
V. 2. only
Refrain
C
F
G
G7
D7

87. Come and go with me

Anon.
Arr. Jeanne Harper

With a happy, light sound
E
A
E
1. Come and go with me ____ to my Fa-ther's house,
B7
E
to my Fa-ther's house, to my Fa-ther's house.
A
E
Come and go with me ____ to my Fa-ther's house where there's
B7
E
joy, ____ joy, ____ joy. ____

2. It's not very far to my Father's house…
3. There is room for all in my Father's house…
4. Everything is free in my Father's house…
5. Jesus is the way to my Father's house…
6. Jesus is the light in my Father's house…

Other verses may be added spontaneously, such as 'We will clap our hands' -- 'There is liberty' -- 'We will praise the Lord' etc., ending with 'Come and go with me.'

88. Ho! everyone that thirsteth

Adapted from Isaiah 55:1-2

Betty Pulkingham

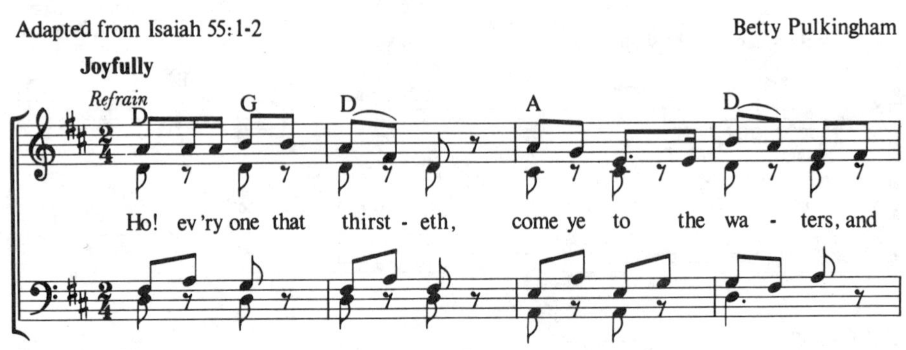

Joyfully
Refrain
D G D A D
Ho! ev'ry one that thirst - eth, come ye to the wa - ters, and

D G D A D
final ending
D
he that hath no mon - ey, come ye, buy and eat. eat.

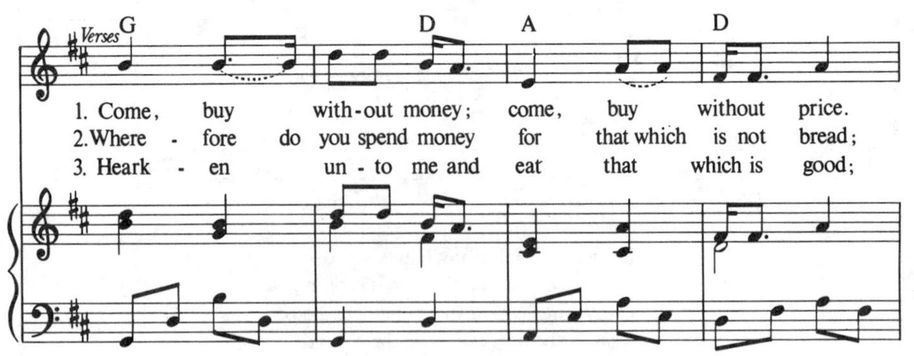

Verses
G D A D
1. Come, buy with-out money; come, buy without price.
2. Where - fore do you spend money for that which is not bread;
3. Heark - en un - to me and eat that which is good;

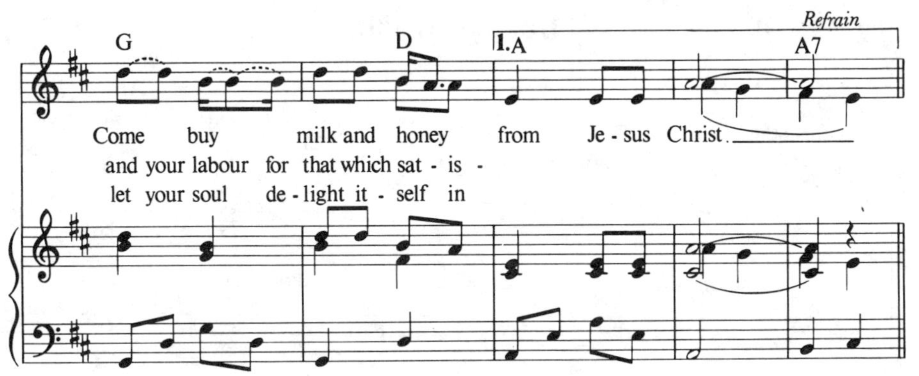
Refrain
G
D
1.A
A7
Come buy milk and honey from Je - sus Christ.
and your labour for that which sat - is -
let your soul de - light it - self in

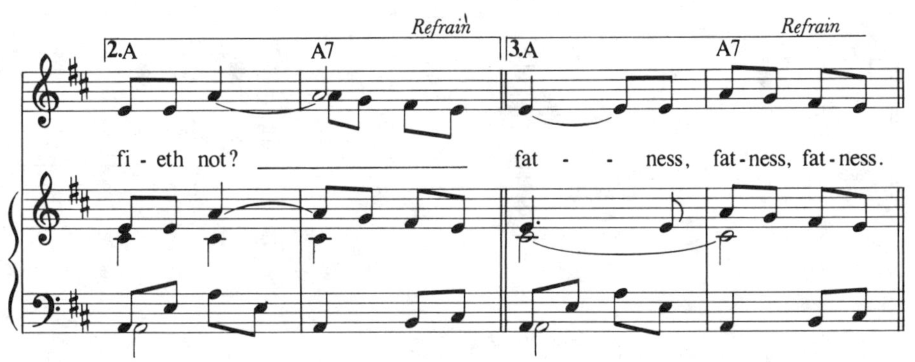
Refrain
Refrain
2.A
A7
3.A
A7
fi - eth not?
fat - - ness, fat-ness, fat-ness.

89. The sea walker

Anon.
Arr. Betty Pulkingham

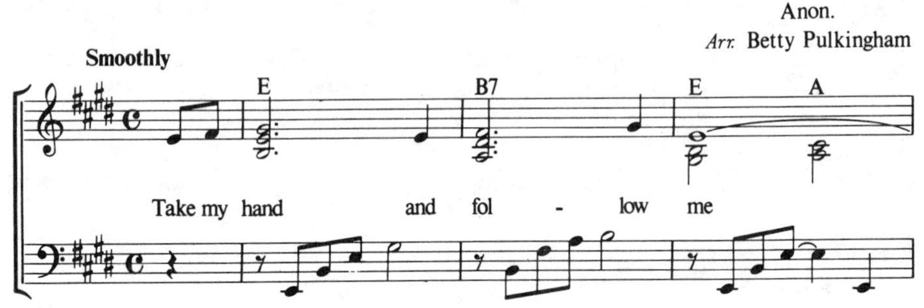
Smoothly
E
B7
E
A
Take my hand and fol - low me

E
Briskly
E
to see the sea wal - ker, the

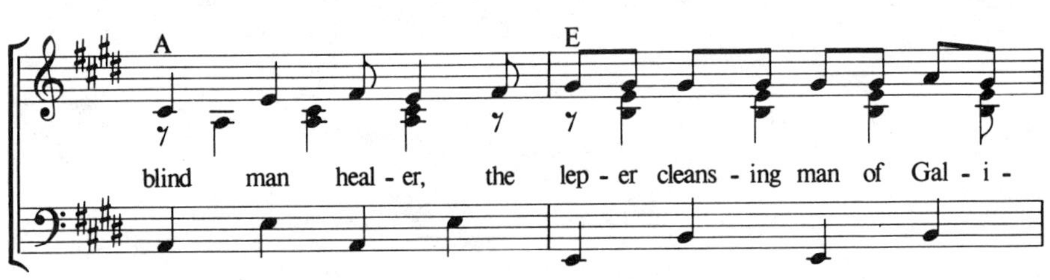
A
E
blind man heal - er, the lep - er cleans - ing man of Gal - i -

B7
E
E7
lee. He's the soul sav - er, the

A E B7
one who set me free, take my hand and fol - low

1.
final ending
E A E E A E
me ___ to see the me.

90. O Lord, all the world belongs to you

Capo 3 (D)

Patrick Appleford
Arr. Jeanne Harper

Smoothly

F(D) C7(A7) F(D) B♭(G) D7(B7)

1. O Lord, all the world be - longs to you, and
2. The world's on - ly lov - ing to its friends, but
3. This world lives di - vid - ed and a - part; you

Gm(Em) D7(B7) Gm(Em) G(E) C(A) C7(A7)

you are al - ways mak - ing all things new. What is
your way of lov - ing ne - ver ends; lov - ing
draw men to - ge - ther and we start in your

F(D) A(F#) Dm(Bm) D7(B7) Gm(Em) D7(B7)
wrong you for - give, and the new life you give is what's
en - em - ies too, and this lov - ing with you is what's
bo - dy to see that in fel - low - ship we can be
F(D) C7(A7) F(D) B♭(G) F(D)
turn-ing the world up - side down.
turn-ing the world up - side down.
turn-ing the world up - side down.

4. The world wants the wealth to live in state,
But you show a new way to be great:
Like a servant you came,
And if we do the same,
We'll be turning the world upside down.

5. O Lord, all the world belongs to you,
And you are always making all things new,
Send your Spirit on all
In your Church whom you call
To be turning the world upside down.

91. Peace is flowing

Anon.
Arr. Betty Pulkingham

Smoothly
E
Peace is flow-ing like a riv - er,
B7
E
Flow - ing out through you and me, ______ Spread - ing out in-to the
des - ert,
B7
E
Set - ting all the cap-tives free.

Other verses may be added:

Love is flowing . . . Joy, Faith, Hope, *etc.*

Optional descant (for 3rd. verse onwards)

92. God is working his purpose out

Arthur Ainger

'Purpose'
Martin Shaw

With breadth
1. God is work - ing his pur - pose out As year suc - ceeds to year: God is work - ing his pur - pose out, And the time is draw - ing near;
2. From ut - most east to ut - most west, Wher - e'er man's foot hath trod, By the mouth of ma - ny mes - sen - gers Goes forth the voice of God;
3. March we forth in the strength of God, With the ban-ner of Christ un - furled, That the light of the glo - rious gos - pel of truth May shine through-out the world;
4. All we can do is noth - ing worth Un - less God bless-es the deed; Vain - ly we hope for the har - vest - tide Till God gives life to the seed; Yet

Near - er and near - er draws the time, The time that shall sure - ly be,
Give ear to me, ye con - ti - nents, Ye isles, give ear to me,
Fight we the fight with sor-row and sin To set their cap - tives free,
near - er and near - er draws the time, The time that shall sure - ly be,
When the earth shall be filled with the glo - ry of God As the wa - ters cov - er the sea.
That the earth may be filled with the glo - ry of God As the wa - ters cov - er the sea.
That the earth may be filled with the glo - ry of God As the wa - ters cov - er the sea.
When the earth shall be filled with the glo - ry of God As the wa - ters cov - er the sea.
Vs. 1, 2, 3.
V. 4.
f

The third stanza may be sung very effectively as a canon, with male voices beginning, treble voices following behind. (See left hand piano part.)

93. Go tell everyone

Alan Dale

Hubert Richards
Arr. Betty Pulkingham

Freely
Am
Verse
Am
1. God's spi - rit is in my
Dm
Am
heart, he has called me and set me a - part.
E
Am
E7
This is what I have to do, what I have to
Brightly
A
Refrain
E7
do: He sent me to give the good news to the
A
E7
poor, tell prisoners that they are prisoners no more; tell

A
D
B7
blind peo - ple that they can see, and set the
E
E7
A
down-trod - den free. And go tell
D
E7
A
ev - 'ry - one the news that the king-dom of God has
A7
D
come, and go tell ev - 'ry - one the
E7
A
E7
A
news that God's king-dom has come.

2. Just as the Father sent me
So I'm sending you out to be
My witness throughout the world
The whole of the world

3. Don't carry a load in your pack,
You don't need two shirts on your back,
A workman can earn his own keep
Can earn his own keep.

4. Don't worry what you have to say,
Don't worry because on that day
God's spirit will speak in your heart,
Will speak in your heart.

94. O Zion, haste

Mary Ann Thompson

'Tidings'
James Walch

Sturdily

1. O Zi - on, haste, thy mis - sion high ful - fill - ing,
2. Pro - claim to ev - 'ry peo - ple, tongue, and na - tion
3. Give of thy sons to bear the mes - sage glo - rious;

To tell to all the world that God is light;
That God, in whom they live and move, is love;
Give of thy wealth to speed them on their way;

That he who made all na - tions is not will - ing
Tell how he stooped to save his lost cre - a - tion,
Pour out thy soul for them in prayer vic - to - rious

One soul should per - ish, lost in shades of night:
And died on earth that man might live a - bove.
Till God shall bring his king-dom's joy - ful day.
Refrain
Pub - lish glad ti - dings: ti - dings of peace,
ti - dings of Je - sus, re - demp - tion and re - lease.

4. He comes again! O Zion, ere thou meet him,
Make known to every heart his saving grace;
Let none whom he hath ransomed fail to greet him,
Through thy neglect, unfit to see his face.

Refrain

95. God has spoken

'Song of good news'

Rev. W. F. Jabusch

Traditional Israeli folk song
Arr. Betty Pulkingham

With vigor
Refrain

Am
E
God has spo - ken to his peo - ple hal - le - lu - jah!

Am
And his words are words of wis - dom, ha - le - lu - jah!

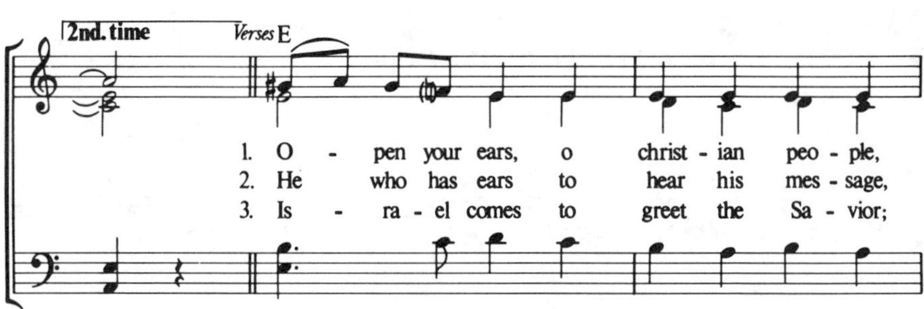
2nd. time
Verses E
1. O - pen your ears, o christ - ian peo - ple,
2. He who has ears to hear his mes - sage,
3. Is - ra - el comes to greet the Sa - vior;

E
O - pen your ears and hear good news. O - pen your hearts, O
He who has ears, then let him hear. He who would learn the
Ju - dah is glad to see his day. From east and west the

Dm
E
Refrain
roy - al priest-hood, God has come to you.
way of wis - dom, let him hear God's word.
peo - ples tra - vel, He will show the way.

The final refrain may be repeated several times as a round, the second part beginning at ~. For additional variety, verses may be sung alternately by male and treble voices.

96. Go forth and tell

Capo 1 (E)

J.E. Seddon | M.A. Baughen

Boldly, with a swing

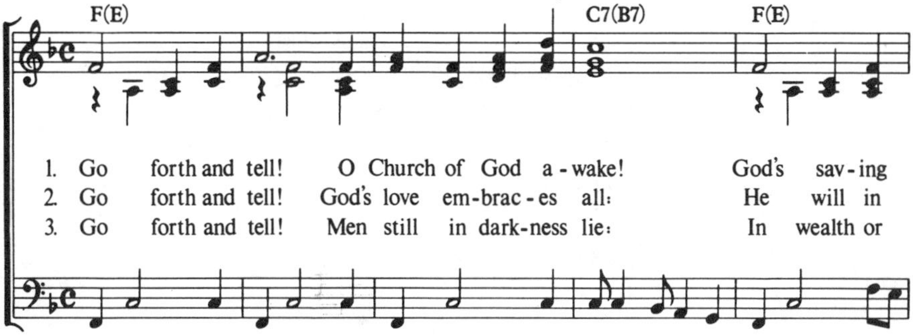

F(E) C7(B7) F(E)

1. Go forth and tell! O Church of God a - wake! God's sav - ing
2. Go forth and tell! God's love em - brac - es all: He will in
3. Go forth and tell! Men still in dark - ness lie: In wealth or

Dm(C♯m) B♭(A) G9 (F♯) C7(B7) F(E) F7(E7)

news to all the na - tions take. Pro - claim Christ Je - sus, Sav - iour
grace res - pond to all who call. How shall they call if they have
want, in sin they live and die. Give us, O Lord, concern of

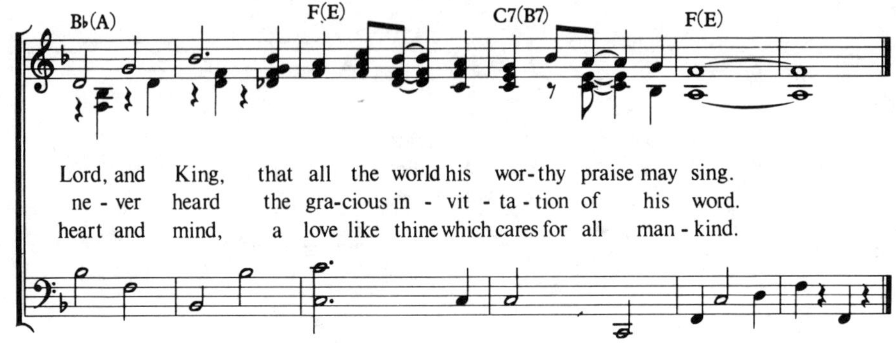

B♭(A)
F(E)
C7(B7)
F(E)
Lord, and King, that all the world his wor-thy praise may sing.
ne - ver heard the gra-cious in - vit - ta - tion of his word.
heart and mind, a love like thine which cares for all man - kind.

4. Go forth and tell! The doors are open wide:
   Share God's good gifts with men so long denied.
 Live out your life as Christ, your Lord, shall choose,
   Your ransomed powers for his sole glory use.

5. Go forth and tell! O Church of God, arise:
   Go in the strength which Christ your Lord supplies.
 Go, till all nations his great name adore
   And serve him Lord and King for evermore.

Sing a Psalm

97. Joy in the Lord

(Psalm 100)

Jane Trigg
Arr. Betty Pulkingham

With a light bounce

Refrain
D A D A D G A7
S
A
(all)
Joy in the Lord, O be joy - ful in the Lord, all ___ ye lands.
T
B

G D G E7 A A7

Serve the Lord with glad-ness. Come be - fore him with a song.
Be sure the Lord is God.___ He has made us, we are his.
O go in - to his courts___ with thanks-giv - ing and praise.
Be thank - ful un - to him,___ and speak good of his name.
The Lord is gra-cious, mer - ci - ful for ev - er - more.

98. Behold, how good and how pleasant it is

(Psalm 133)

Capo 3 (A)

Kathleen Thomerson
Arr. Betty Pulkingham

Calypso style

Be - hold how good and how plea - sant it
is for breth - ren to dwell to-geth - er in
un - i - ty.
1. It is like
2. As the dew
3. For there

the prec – ious oint – ment u – pon the head that ran
of Her – mon and as the dew that des –
the Lord com – mand ed, com–
down up – on the beard, even Aaron's
cend – ed up on the moun – of Zi – on,
mand – – – ed the bless – ing.
verse 3
beard, that ran down to the skirts of his gar – ments;
For there the Lord com – mand – ed
Ev – en

1
2
3rd (& final) ending
Be bless ing. Be life
for. ev – er – more.

99. The Lord has done great things for us

(Psalm 126)
Music by Eleven: fifty-nine
Arr. Betty Pulkingham
Soft rock
Introduction
Verse
E
1. When the Lord re-stored the for-tunes of Zi on, we were like those who
said a-mong the na-tions, 'The Lord has done great things for
store our for-tunes, O Lord, as the wa-ter cours-es in the
goes forth weep-ing bear-ing the seed for
Bm7
E
Verse 2

dream. Then our mouths were filled with
Ne - geb. May those who sow in
sow - ing, shall come home with shouts of
laugh - ter, and our tongues with shouts of
tears, reap with shouts of
joy, bring - ing his sheaves
Refrain
joy!
joy! The Lord has done great things for
with him.

us, and we are glad.
1
The Lord has done
2
2. Then they
3. Re -
4. He that
final

100 The Lord hath put a new song

(Psalm 40)

Mimi Armstrong Farra

Joyfully
Refrain
D G D
The Lord hath put a new song in my
A D
mouth, in my mouth, in my mouth. The
G
Lord hath put a new song in my mouth,
A D G D
ev - en praise un - to our God.

G
Verses may be sung as solo
D
1. And ma-ny shall __ see it and fear and trust,
2. I de - light to do thy will, oh God, thy
3. I have not hid thy right-eous-ness with - in my heart, with-
4. I've not con-cealed thy lov-ing kind-ness and thy truth,
5. So let thy ___ lov-ing kind-ness and thy truth,
6. Let all those that seek thee re - joice and be glad, re-
A
D
fear and trust, fear and trust. And
will, oh God, thy will, oh God.
in my heart, with - in my heart. I
and thy truth, and thy truth, I've
and thy truth, and thy truth, so
joice and be glad, re - joice and be glad. Let

G
D
ma - ny shall ___ see it and fear and trust,
I de - light to do thy will, oh God. Thy
have not hid thy right-eous-ness with - in my heart.
not con - cealed thy lov - ing kind-ness and thy_ truth,
let thy ___ lov - ing kind-ness and thy_ truth con-
all those that seek thee re - joice and be glad, re-
A
A7
D
G
D
Refrain
and shall trust in the Lord.
law is with - in my ___ heart.
I have de - clared thy sal - va - tion.
from the great con - gre - ga - tion.
tin - u - al - ly pre - serve me.
joice and be glad in ___ thee.

101. As a doe

(Psalm 42)

Capo 2 (Am)

Mike Fitzgerald
Arr. Mimi Farra

Sustained, without dragging
Refrain
Bm(Am)
Em(Dm)
As a doe longs for run-ning
Bm(Am)
streams, so longs my soul for
F♯7(E7)
Bm(Am)
1,3
Verse
you, my God.
1. My soul is
3. Why so

Em(Dm)
thirst - ing for the God of life;
down - cast, O my soul?
Bm(Am)
F♯(E)
F♯7(E7)
when shall I see him face to face?
Why do you sigh so deep with - in?
Bm(Am)
Em(Dm)
I have no food but tears day and
Place your hope in the God of

Bm(Am)
F♯7(E7)
Bm(Am)
night; ___ and men say, 'Where is your God?'
life. ___ I ___ shall praise him a - gain.
Refrain
2,4
G(F)
2. I ___ re - mem-ber and my
4. When I find my soul ___
D(C)
G(F)
soul melts with - in. I'm on my
down - cast with - in, I think of

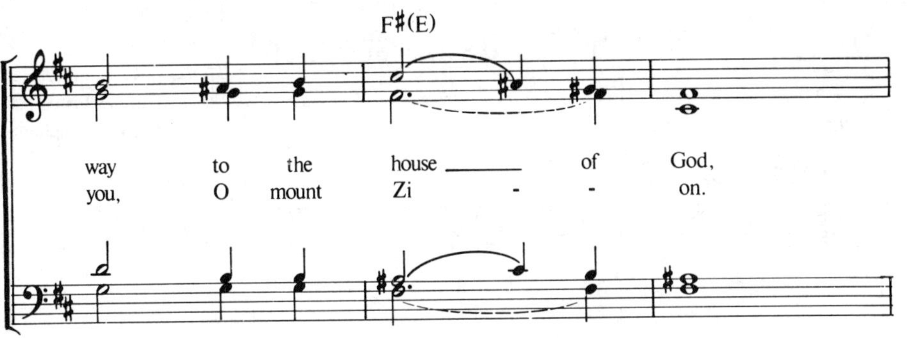
F♯(E)
way to the house ___ of God,
you, O mount Zi - - on.

G(F)
D(C)
a - mong cries ___ of joy ___ and praise;
Deep calls to deep as your wa - ters roar;

Bm(Am)
F♯7(E7)
Bm(Am)
Refrain
place ___ your trust ___ in God.
ov - er me all your waves pour.

102. The Lord's my shepherd

Psalm 23
Scottish Psalter

Jessie Seymour Irvine
Arr. Thomas Pritchard
Descant Betty Pulkingham

Flowing
Descant
2. My soul he doth
3. My ta - ble thou hast
1. The Lord's my shep - herd, I'll not
2. My soul he doth re - store a -
3. Yea, though I walk in death's dark

re-store a-gain And me to walk doth make
fur-nish-ed In pre-sence of my foes.
want; He makes me down to lie In
gain; And me to walk doth make With-
vale, Yet will I fear none ill: For

The paths of right-eous-ness, e'en for
My head thou dost with oil a - noint
pas - tures green; he lead - eth me The
in the paths of right - eous - ness, E'en
thou art with me; and thy rod And

his own name's sake.
and my cup ov - er flows.
qui - et wa - ters by.
for his own name's sake.
staff me com - fort still.

4. My table thou hast furnished
 In presence of my foes;
My head thou dost with oil anoint,
 And my cup overflows.

5. Goodness and mercy all my life
 Shall surely follow me:
And in God's house for evermore
 My dwelling-place shall be.

103. Sing a new song to the Lord

Timothy Dudley-Smith
David G. Wilson
With a swing
G F G F
1. Sing a new song to the Lord,
2. Now to the ends of the earth
3. Sing a new song and re - joice,
G Dm G F
He to whom won - ders be - long! Re -
See his sal - va - tion is shown! And
Pub - lish his prai - ses a - broad! Let
Em A
joice in his tri - umph and
still he re - mem - bers his
voi - ces in chor - us, with
Em F D7
tell of his power, O
mer - cy and truth, Un -
trum - pet and horn, Re -

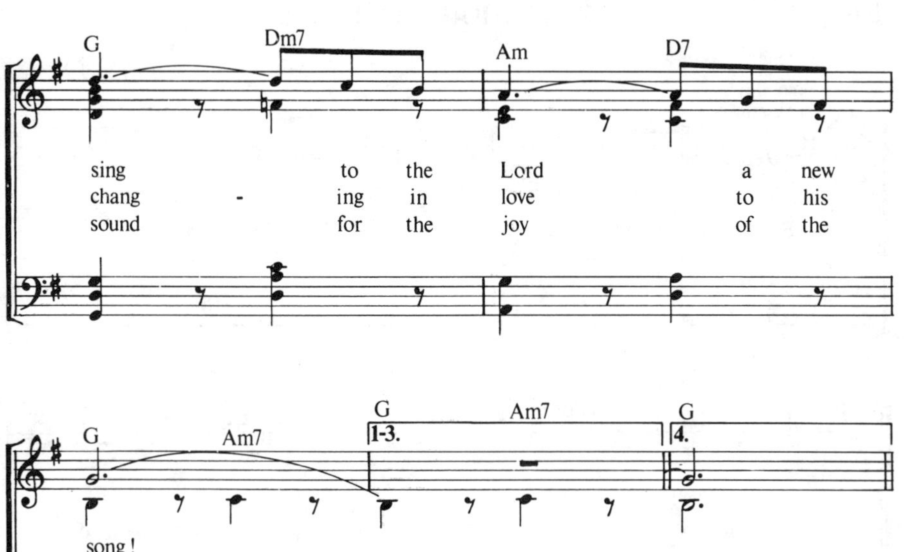
G
Dm7
Am
D7
sing to the Lord a new
chang - ing in love to his
sound for the joy of the

G Am7 G Am7 G

1-3. 4.

song!
own.
Lord!

4. Join with the hills and the sea
Thunders of praise to prolong!
In judgement and justice he comes to the earth,
O sing to the Lord a new song!

104. Bless thou the Lord

Betty Pulkingham

Smoothly
D Refrain
Bless thou the Lord, O my soul,
A
D
bless thou the Lord, O my soul.
Bless thou the Lord,
O my soul, and for - get not all his ben - e -
D
1-5
D
final ending
fits.
1. Who for -
2. Who re -
3. The
fits.

G
Verses
D
giv - eth all thine in - i - qui-ties, who
deem - eth thy life from de - struc - tion, who
Lord is mer - ci - ful and gra - cious, slow to

A7
D
A7
heal - eth all thy dis - eas - es.
crown - eth thee with lov - ing kind - ness.
an - ger and plen - teous in mer - cy.

4. For as the heaven is high above the earth,
   So great his mercy toward them that fear him.

5. Like as a father pitieth his children,
   So the Lord pitieth them that fear him.

105. I rejoiced when I heard them say

(Psalm 122)

Betty Pulkingham

Joyfully
Refrain
A D E A D E A
last time
I re - joiced when I heard them say,
'Let us go to God's house to - day!'
I re-joiced when I heard them say,
'Let us go to God's house.'

D
A
1. And now our
2. Je - ru - sa - lem is
3. For the peace of Je -
4. For love of my
E7
A
feet ___ are stand - ing, stand - ing with -
built as a ci - ty, it ___ is
ru - - sa - lem pray, peace be to your
breth - - ren and friends, for love of the
D
A
in thy gates, O Je -
there that the tribes go up, the
homes peace to your
house of the Lord, I will say,

E7
A
Ref
ru - - - sa lem.
tribes of the Lord.
homes - al - way.
Peace peace up - on you.'
E
A
E
Let us go to God's house.
Let us go
E7
A
A
Refrain
to God's house.

Come as Children . . .
Songs for children of all ages

106. The butterfly song

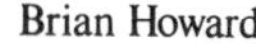
Brian Howard

Playfully

D G

1. If I were a but - ter - fly, I'd thank you, Lord, for
2. If I were an e - le - phant, I'd thank you, Lord, by
3. If I were a wig - gily worm, I'd thank you, Lord, that

D

giv - ing me wings. And if I were a ro - bin in a tree, I'd
rais - ing my trunk. And if I were a kan - ga - roo, you
I could squirm. And if I were a bil - ly - goat, I'd

A A7 D

thank you, Lord, that I could sing. And if I were a
know I'd hop right up to you. And if I were an
thank you, Lord, for my strong throat. And if I were a

G

fish in the sea, I'd wig - gle my tail and I'd
oct - o - pus, I'd thank you, Lord, for
fuz - zy - wuz - zy bear, I'd thank you, Lord, for my

A
gig - gle with glee, but
my fine looks, but
fuz - zy-wuz-zy hair, but
I just thank you, Fa-ther, for mak - ing me
D G D
'me.' For you gave me a heart and you
G
gave me a smile. You gave me Je - sus and you made me your child. And
A
D G D
I just thank you, Fa-ther, for mak-ing me 'me.'

A good song to stimulate a child's imagination. Verse 3 was added by children from a multi-racial, inner-city school.

107. Jesus, Jesus is my Lord

John Franklin (age 12)
Betty Pulkingham
Cheerfully
Refrain
1
Je - sus, Je - sus is my Lord; al-ways o-bey what Je - sus says.
2
Je - sus says.
Verses
1. That's the way to lay down your life,
2. He re - wards you, mak-ing you free,
3. He has giv-en his Spi-rit to you,
al-ways o-bey what Je - sus says.
The ones who come for
And then you have pow-er ov-er the
So keep his words and
Je - sus' life,
en - e - my,
he will keep you,
al-ways o-bey what Je - sus says.
Refrain

108. The Lord is my shepherd

(2-part round)
Adapted from Psalm 23
Capo 1 (E)
Anon.
Arr. Betty Pulkingham
Smoothly flowing
1
F(E) C7(B7) F(E)
The Lord is my Shep-herd, I'll fol-low Him al-way, He
F(E) C7(B7) F(E)
leads me by still wa-ters, I'll fol-low Him al-way. Al-
2
F(E) C7(B7) F(E)
way, al-way, I'll fol-low Him al-way. Al-way, al-
Lord is my Shep-herd, I'll fol-low Him al-way. He leads me by still
F(E) C7(B7) 1 F(E) 2 F(E)
way, I'll fol-low Him al-way, The
wa-ter, I'll fol-low Him al- Al-way.

109. Oh, how I love Jesus

Capo 1 (E)

Refrain: F. Whitfield
Arr. Betty Pulkingham

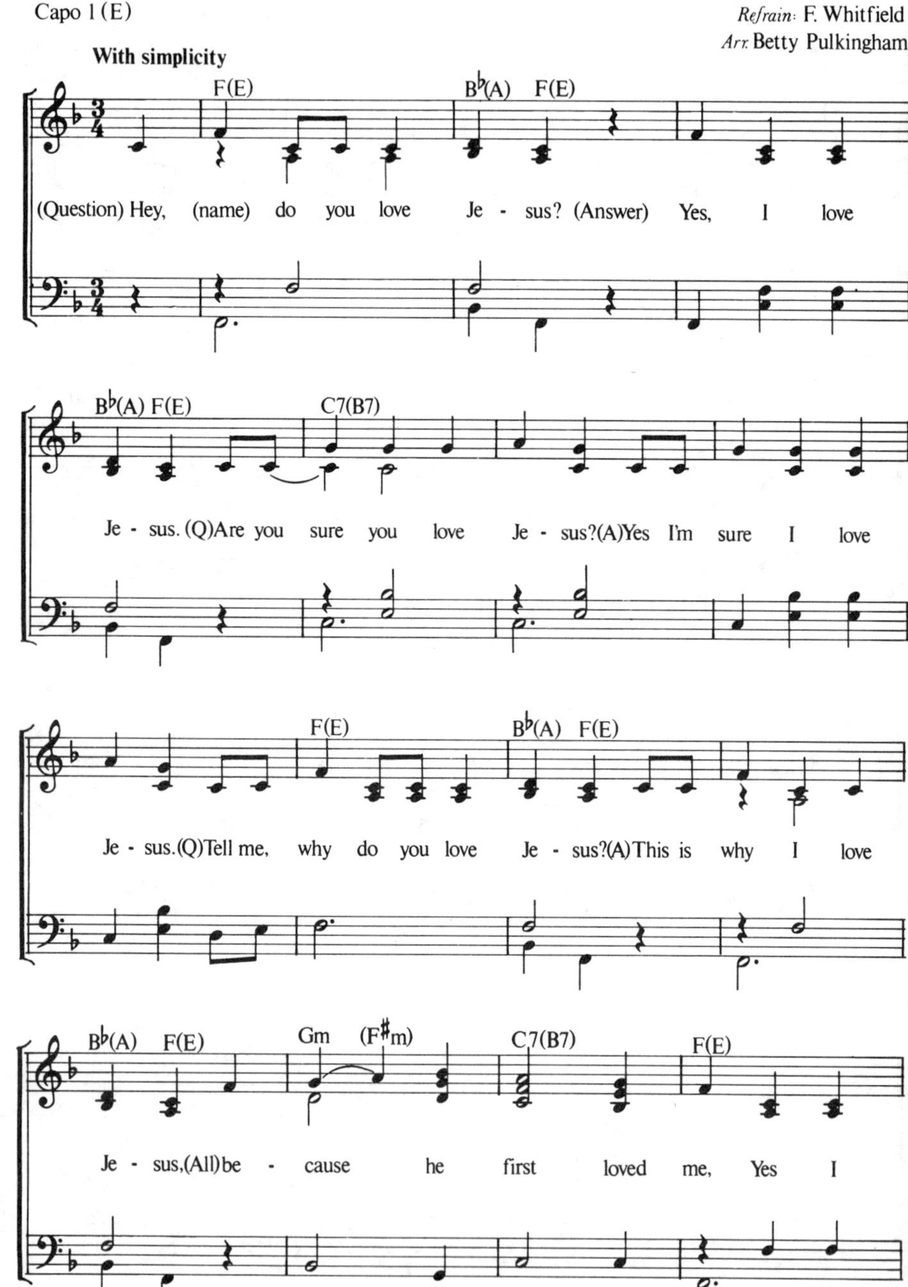
With simplicity
F(E)
B♭(A) F(E)
(Question) Hey, (name) do you love Je - sus? (Answer) Yes, I love
B♭(A) F(E)
C7(B7)
Je - sus. (Q)Are you sure you love Je - sus?(A)Yes I'm sure I love
F(E)
B♭(A) F(E)
Je - sus.(Q)Tell me, why do you love Je - sus?(A)This is why I love
B♭(A) F(E)
Gm (F♯m)
C7(B7)
F(E)
Je - sus,(All)be - cause he first loved me, Yes I

B♭(A) F(E)
B♭(A) F(E)
Refrain:
F(E)
love him, this is why I love him Oh,
C7 (B7)
how I love Je - sus, Oh,
F(E)
F(E)
how I love Je - sus, Oh,
Gm (F♯m)
how I love Je - sus, be - cause he

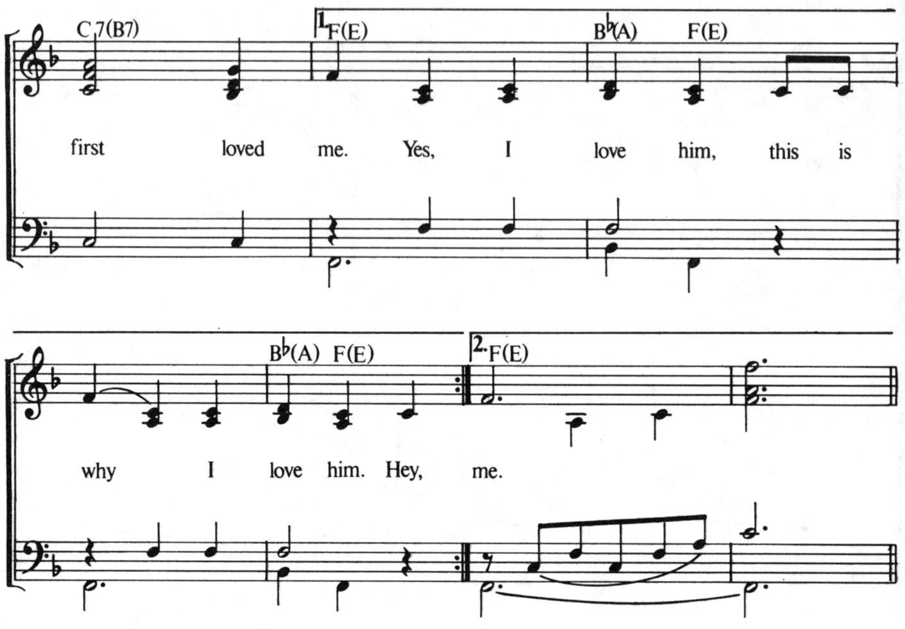
C 7(B7)
1. F(E)
B♭(A) F(E)
first loved me. Yes, I love him, this is
B♭(A) F(E)
2. F(E)
why I love him. Hey, me.

The first part of this song is a dialogue. One person starts it and the one who is named sings the answers, and in turn asks the questions the second time round.
A good concluding verse is 'Hey saints' (or 'family' or 'kids') - - - some term which includes all of those present.

110. Praise the Lord

"Sing, sing, praise and sing"

Elizabeth Syré

With a swing

Refrain
F
C7
F
Sing, sing, praise and sing! Hon - our God for ev - ery - thing.

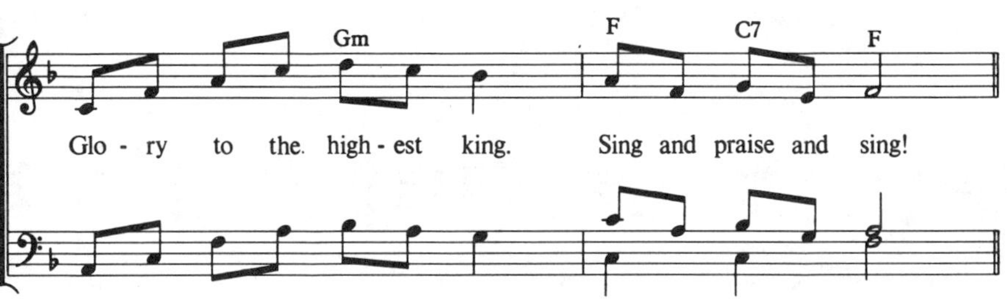

Gm
F
C7
F
Glo - ry to the high - est king. Sing and praise and sing!

Verses
C
F
G7
C
C7
1. Clap your hands, lift your voice, praise the Lord and re - joice!
2. Full of joy, full of rest, in our Lord we are blessed.
3. Are you weak? Ne - ver mind! Come and sing, "God is kind!"

4. Love and peace is so near.
   Praise the Lord!
   God can hear!

5. Cymbal, harp, violin,
   Angels, priests,
   All join in.

111.

The body song

Adapted from I Cor. 12. 14-26

Betty Pulkingham

Sprightly

D
1. If the eye say to the hand, I have no need of thee. or the
2. If the foot shall say, Be-cause I'm not the hand, I
3. If the ear shall say, Be-cause I'm not the eye, I

A
head to the feet, I have no need of you. Well, oh
don't feel like a handsome part. Well, oh
don't seem to see things ve – ry clear – – – ly. Well, oh

D
how can we write or hold a thim-ble? How can we walk or run so nim-ble?
what does it matter to be first or to be latter? God has
where were the hearing, and oh where were the smelling if the

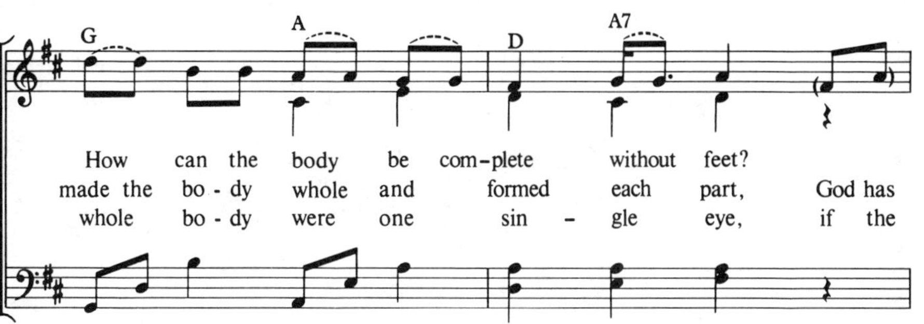
G
A
D
A7
How can the body be com-plete without feet?
made the bo - dy whole and formed each part, God has
whole bo - dy were one sin - gle eye, if the

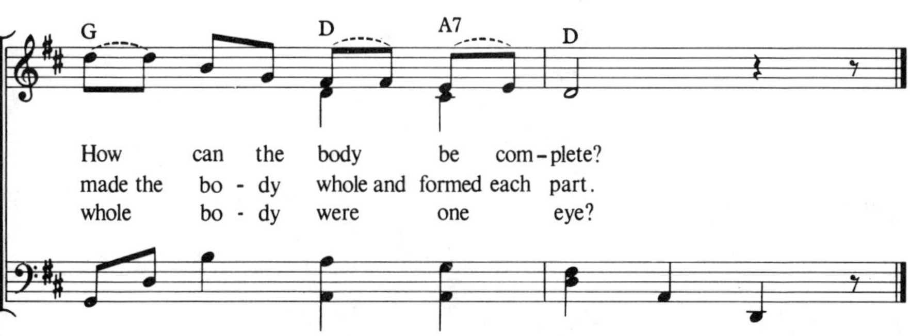
G
D
A7
D
How can the body be com-plete?
made the bo - dy whole and formed each part.
whole bo - dy were one eye?

4. One / single 'I', it cannot be a body.
   One / single 'you' a body? 'Nay!'
Oh,/God hath set the members,
   They are / many, many members,
Yet one / body as it pleased him are they.
   Yet one / body as it pleased him are they.

This is a good action song: point to the eye, the hand, etc. as they are mentioned.

112. We love the Lord

'David's song'

David Pulkingham
(Age 4)

Slowly and quietly

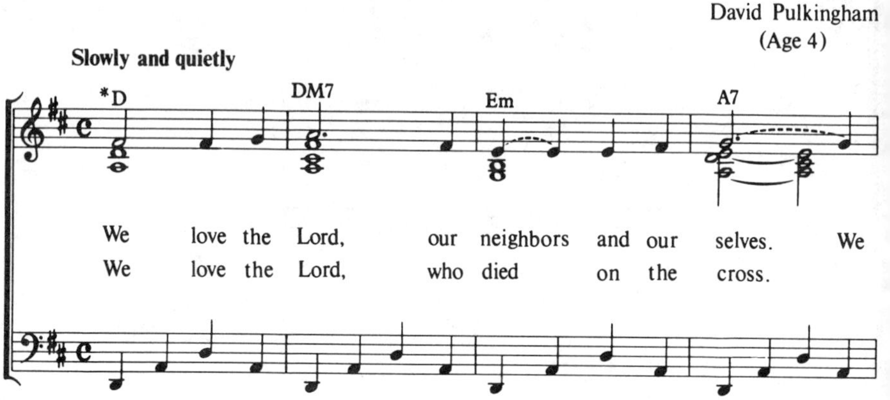

*D
DM7
Em
A7
We love the Lord, our neighbors and our selves. We
We love the Lord, who died on the cross.

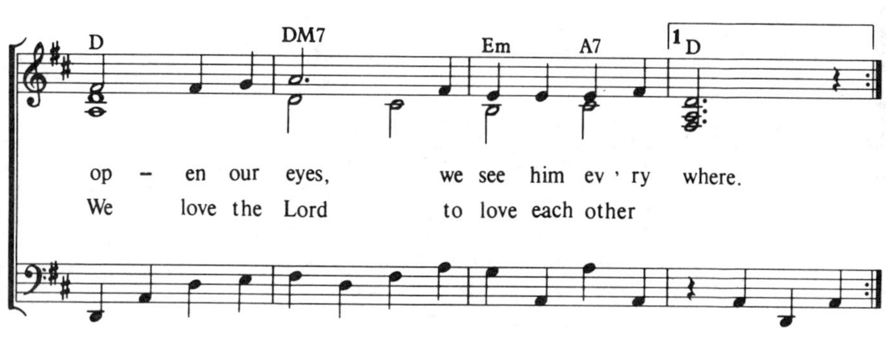

D
DM7
Em
A7
1 D
op – en our eyes, we see him ev'ry where.
We love the Lord to love each other

2 D
DM7
Em
too. We op - en our eyes, we see Je-sus,

A7
D
DM7
Em
Christ; he looks down at us, we look up at

A7
D
DM7
Em
A7
D
him. We trust in him e - ter - nal - ly.

Children of all ages enjoy singing this song with graceful and simple motions: 'We' (hands pointing to self) 'love the Lord' (hands lifted up), 'our neighbors' (hands circling outwards) 'and ourselves' (back to self). 'We open our eyes' (hands over eyes, then opening like gates swinging open), 'we see him everywhere' (same as 'neighbors'). 'We love the Lord' (as above) 'who died on the cross' (forearms crossed). 'We love the Lord' (as above) 'to love each other too' (same as 'neighbors'). 'We open our eyes' (repeat above), 'we see Jesus Christ' (looking up), 'he looks down at us' (looking and extending arms down), 'we look up at him' (looking and extending arms up). 'We trust in him eternally' (arms in encircling motion).

113. Thank you, Lord

Capo 1(E)

Diane Davis

Bouncy
F(E)
Bb(A)
F(E)
1. Thank you, Lord, for this fine day. Thank
Al - - le - lu - ia, praise the Lord. Al -

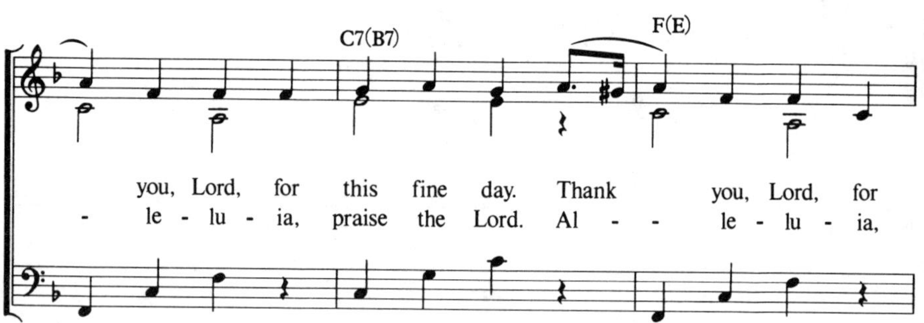
C7(B7)
F(E)
you, Lord, for this fine day. Thank you, Lord, for
- le - lu - ia, praise the Lord. Al - - le - lu - ia,

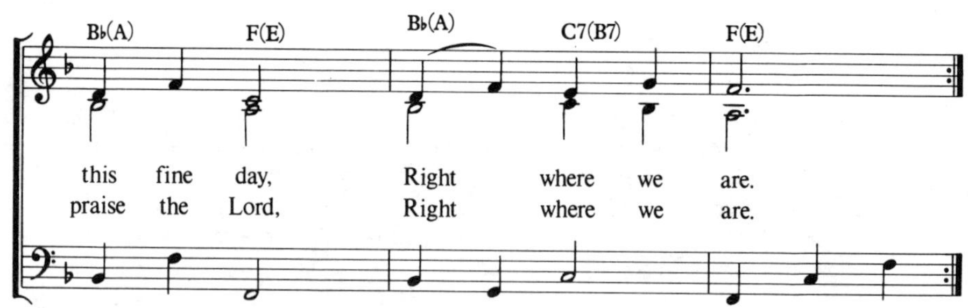
Bb(A)
F(E)
Bb(A)
C7(B7)
F(E)
this fine day, Right where we are.
praise the Lord, Right where we are.

2. Thank you, Lord, for loving us.
3. Thank you, Lord, for giving us peace.
4. Thank you, Lord, for setting us free.
5. Thank you, Lord, for games to play.

114. # Jesus is a friend of mine

Paul Mazak *(Age4)*
Arr. Betty Pulkingham

With childlike simplicity

E
B7
A
B7
1. Je - sus is a friend of mine, praise
E
B7
E
B7
him. Praise him. Je - sus is a
E
A
B7
E
rit.
friend of mine, praise him.

2. Jesus died to set us free, praise him.

3. He gave us the victory, praise him.

4. Jesus is the King of kings, praise him.

115. The wedding banquet

Str. Miriam Therese Winter
Arr. Betty Pulkingham

Lively
Refrain
D
D7
G
I can - not come. I can - not come to the
D
A7
ban - quet, don't trou - ble me now. I have mar - ried a
D
D7
G
wife, I have bought me a cow. I have fields and com
D
A7
- mitments that cost a pret - ty sum. Pray, hold me ex - cused, I can - not

'The wedding banquet' available on album AVS 101 from Avant Garde Records, Inc. 250 W. 57th St., N.Y., or 12 Portland Road, London, England.

Verses
G
A cer - tain man held a
The mas - ter rose up in
When all the poor had as -
Now God has writ - ten a
D
come.
D
feast on his fine es - tate in town, he
an - ger, called his ser - vants by name, said: "Go
- sem - bled, there was still room to spare, so the
les - son for the rest of man - kind; if
A
A7
D
laid a fes - tive ta - ble and wore a wed - ding
in - to the town, fetch the blind and the
mas - ter de - man - ded: "Go search ev - 'ry -
we're slow in res - pond - ing, he may leave us be -

D7
gown. He sent in - vi - ta - tions to his
lame, fetch the pea - sant and the pau - per, for
where, to the high - ways and the by - ways, and
hind. He's pre - par - ing a ban - quet for that
D
A
neigh - bors far and wide, but when the meal was
this I have willed, my ban - quet must be
force them to come in. My ta - ble must be
great and glo - rious day. When the Lord and Mas - ter
A7
D
Refrain
rea - dy, each of them re - plied:
crow - ded, and my ta - ble must be filled."
filled be - fore the ban - quet can be - gin."
calls us, be cer - tain not to say:
D.C.

Songs for a Season

116. Wake up!

Betty Pulkingham

Lightly and sprightly
Refrain
D
G
A7
Wake up! Wake up! It's time to rise and sing the praise of
D
G
A
A7
D
G
Je - sus, al - le-lu, al - le - lu - ia. It's time to rise, to sing, to
A
G
F♯m
G
shout, to bring him all your heart. He'll do the big - ger
D
A
A7
D
part, if you will on - ly make a start.

G D C D
In the days of No - ah's fam - i - ly, the peo - ple
John came bap - tiz - ing in the wil - der - ness;
When Je - sus came to John in the wil - der - ness; John said,
Je - sus told a sto - ry of ten mai - dens fair;
What good is a lamp with - out an - y oil?
G D C D verse 5
didn't know what the score was e - ter - nal - ly. They
preach - ing to those who their sins con - fessed. But to
'I should be the one to come to you, I must con - fess! For
five were wise and rea - dy, five did not pre - pare. Those
What good is our life if we strug - gle and toil, but
G D C D
ate, and drank, got mar - ried and then their
those who came for strife and de - bate, he said,
I bap - tize with wa - ter at the most, but
girls had lamps, but oh, dear me! They

G
D
C
D
Refrain
sons and their daughters did the same things a - gain.
'Who told you to come here, you tribe of snakes?'
you will bap - tize with the Ho - ly Ghost!'
had no oil to light them so that they could see.
G
verse 5
D
C
D
can - not see God's king - dom here, and
G
D
C
D
Refrain
live the loving life of his son so dear?

117. On Jordan's bank

Charles Coffin
Tr. John Chandler

Gary Miles
Arr. Betty Pulkingham

With vigor
1. On Jor - dan's bank the Bap - tist's cry
2. Then cleansed be ev - 'ry breast from sin;
3. For thou art our sal - va - tion, Lord,
An - noun - ces that the Lord is nigh; A-
Make straight the way for God with - in, And
Our re - fuge, and our great re - ward; With-
wake and heark - en, for he brings Glad ti - dings of the
let each heart pre - pare a home Where such a mighty
out thy grace we waste a - way Like flowers that with - er
King of kings.
guest may come.
and de - cay.
final ending

4. To heal the sick stretch out thine hand,
And bid the fallen sinner stand;
Shine forth, and let thy light light restore
Earth's own true lovliness.

5. All praise, eternal Son, to thee,
Whose advent doth thy people free;
Whom with the Father we adore
And Holy Ghost for evermore.

118. Calypso carol

Michael Perry
Arr. Stephen Coates

Liltingly
D
G
1. See him a - ly - ing on a bed of straw;
2. Star of sil - ver sweep a - cross the skies,
3. An - gels, sing - a - gain the song you sang,
A7
D
draugh - ty sta - ble with an op - en door,
show where Je - sus in the man - ger lies.
bring God's glo - ry to the heart of man;
D
G
Em
Ma - ry cra - dl - ing the babe she bore; The
Shep - herds swift - ly from your stu - por rise to
Sing that Bethl' - hem's litt - le ba - by can
A7
D
D7
prince of glo - ry is his name.
see the Sav - iour of the world.
be sal - va - tion to the soul.

Refrain:
G
D
Oh, now car - ry me to Beth - le - hem to
A7
D
see the Lord a - ppear to men;
B7
Em
Just as poor as was the sta - ble then, The
A7
Verses 1-3
Verse 4
D Gm D Gm D
prince of glo - ry when he came.

4. Mine are riches from thy poverty,
From thine innocence, eternity;
Mine, forgiveness by thy death for me,
Child of sorrow for my joy.

119. Oh, Mary, don't you weep

Mimi Farra

Gently rocking
Refrain Cm (Am)
Oh, Ma - ry don't you weep
Fm (Dm)
1. Cm (Am)
and Ma-ry don't you cry.
2. Cm (Am) Gm(Em) Cm(Am)
cry.
3.4. Cm (Am) Gm(Em)
cry.
Cm(Am)
Fine

Cm(Am)
1. Oh, lit - tle ba - by Je sus,
2. Ba - by Je - sus is gon - na die
3. Oh, sing glo - ry hal - le - lu - jah,

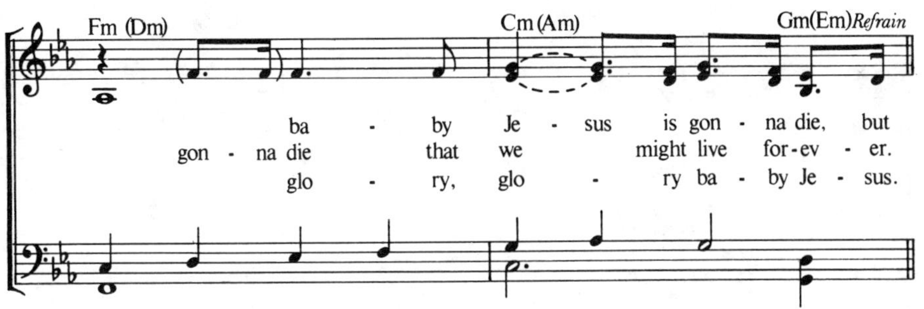
Fm (Dm)
Cm (Am)
Gm(Em) Refrain
ba - by Je - sus is gon - na die, but
gon - na die that we might live for - ev - er.
glo - ry, glo - ry ba - by Je - sus.

120. See, amid the winter's snow

Edward Caswall

'Humility'
John Goss

Tenderly
Solo or unison
1. See a - mid the win ter's snow, born for us on
2. Lo, with - in a man - ger lies he who built the
3. Say, ye ho - ly shep - herds, say, what your joy - ful
earth be - low see the ten - der lamb ap-pears,
star - ry skies, he who, throned in height sub-lime,
news to - day; where - fore have ye left your sheep
prom - ised from et - er - nal years.
sits a - mid the cher - u - bim.
on the lone - ly moun - tain steep?
Refrain
Hail, thou e - ver
bless - ed morn! Hail re - demp - tion's hap - py dawn!

Sing through all Jer - us - a - lem: Christ is born in Beth - le - hem.

4. 'As we watched at dead of night,
Lo, we saw a wondrous light:
Angels, singing peace on earth,
Told us of the Saviour's birth.'

5. Sacred infant, all divine,
What a tender love was thine,
Thus to come from highest bliss
Down to such a world as this!

6. Teach, O teach us, holy child,
By thy face so meek and mild,
Teach us to resemble thee
In thy sweet humility.

121. Go tell it on the mountain

North American spiritual
Arr. Betty Pulkingham

Flowing

Refrain
*G
CM7
G
Am
D7
Go tell it on the moun - tain, ov - er the hills and

G
D
G
CM7
G
ev - 'ry where. Go tell it on the moun - tain that

CM7
D7
G
Fine
Verses
G
Je - sus Christ is born.
1. While shep - herds kept their
2. The shep - herds feared and
3. Down in a low - ly

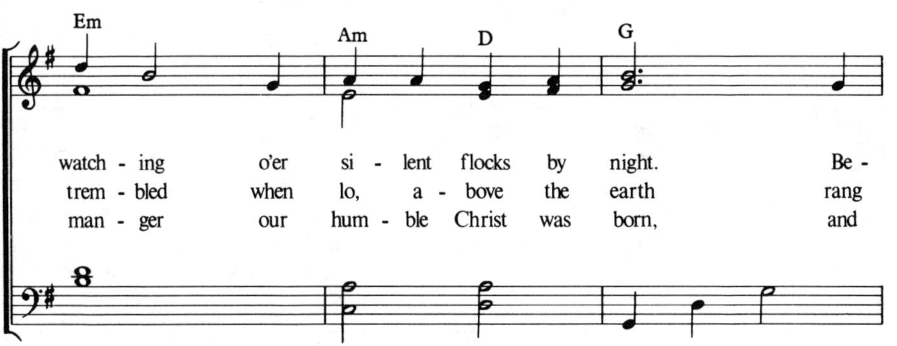
Em
Am
D
G
watch - ing o'er si - lent flocks by night. Be -
trem - bled when lo, a - bove the earth rang
man - ger our hum - ble Christ was born, and

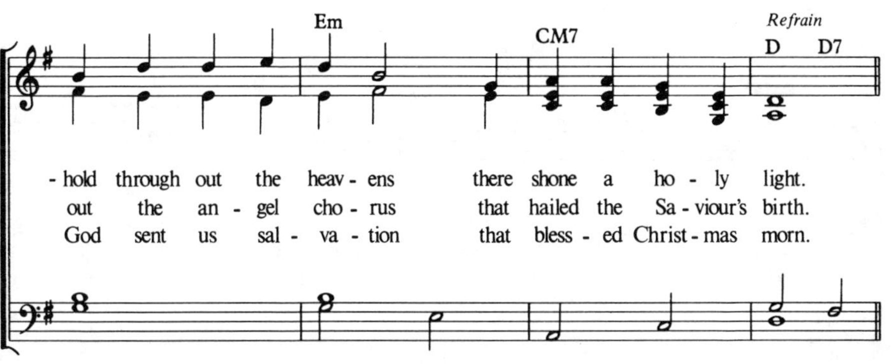
Em
CM7
Refrain
D D7
- hold through out the heav - ens there shone a ho - ly light.
out the an - gel cho - rus that hailed the Sa - viour's birth.
God sent us sal - va - tion that bless - ed Christ - mas morn.

4. When I was a seeker, I sought both night and day;
   I asked the Lord to help me, and he showed me the way.

5. He made me a watchman upon the city wall,
   And if I am a Christian, I am the least of all.

122. Let your light shine

Shirley Lewis Brown

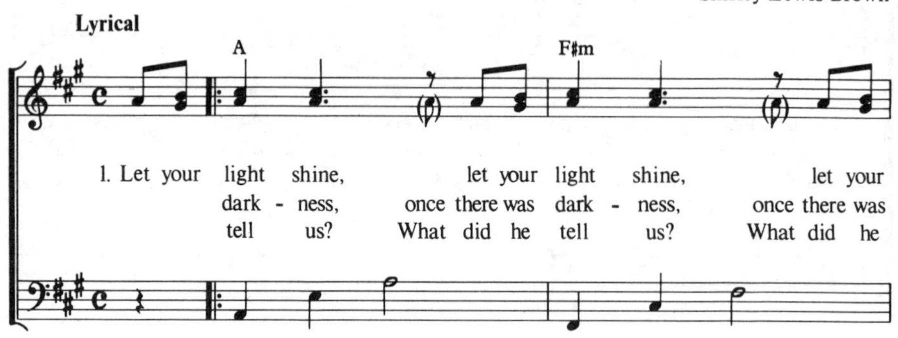
Lyrical
A
F♯m
1. Let your light shine, let your light shine, let your
dark - ness, once there was dark - ness, once there was
tell us? What did he tell us? What did he

DM7
A
light shine be - fore men, that they may
dark - ness up - on earth. Then God sent
tell us we should do? He said to

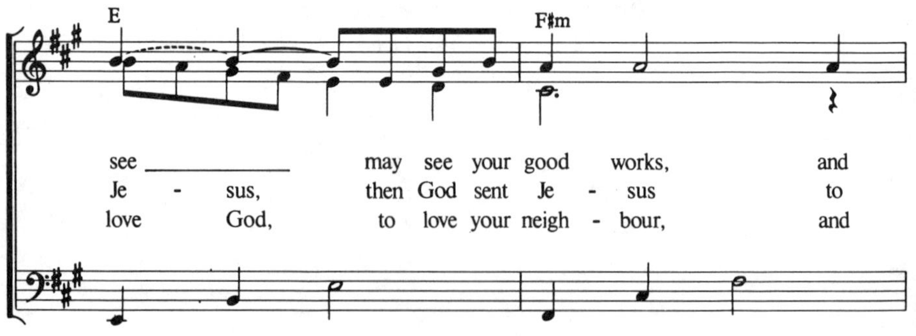
E
F♯m
see ___ may see your good works, and
Je - sus, then God sent Je - sus to
love God, to love your neigh - bour, and

Bm
E
glo - - - ri - fy the
light the way, the
serve him let your

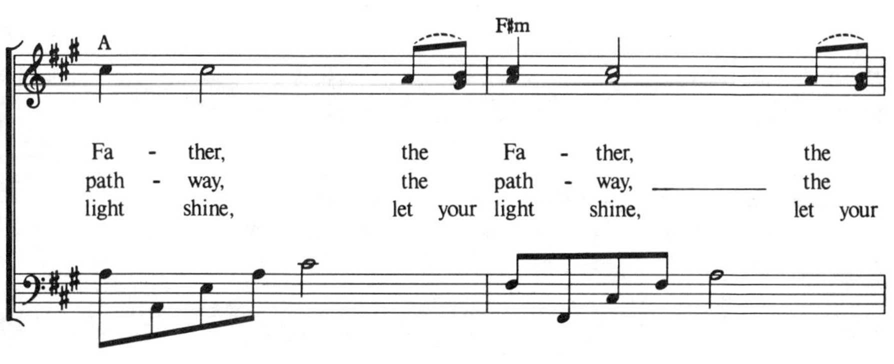
A
F♯m
Fa - ther, the Fa - ther, the
path - way, the path - way, the
light shine, let your light shine, let your

DM7
last time
A
A
Fa - ther who is in heav'n. 2. Once there was
path - way back to God. 3. What did he
light shine be - fore men.

123. Wondrous love

Traditional North American Melody

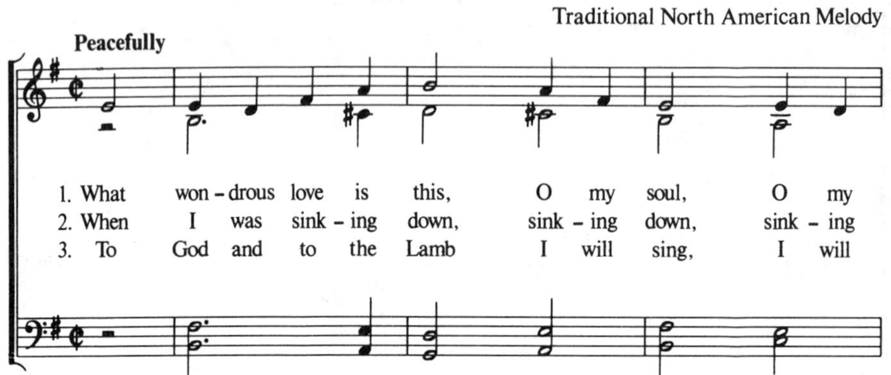
Peacefully
1. What won - drous love is this, O my soul, O my
2. When I was sink - ing down, sink - ing down, sink - ing
3. To God and to the Lamb I will sing, I will

soul? What won - drous love is this, O my soul? What
down, When I was sink - ing down, sink - ing down, When
sing. To God and to the Lamb I will sing. To

won-drous love is this that caused the Lord of bliss To
I was sink - ing down be - neath God's right - eous frown, Christ
God and to the Lamb who is the great I AM, While

bear the dread - ful curse for my soul, for my soul, To
laid a - side his crown for my soul, for my soul, Christ
thou-sands join the theme, I will sing, I will sing, While

1
2
bear the dread - ful curse for my soul.
laid a - side his crown for my soul.
join the theme, I will sing.

4. And when from death I'm free, I'll sing on. I'll sing on,
And when from death I'm free, I'll sing on.
And when from death I'm free, I'll sing and joyful be,
And through eternity I'll sing on. I'll sing on,
And through eternity I'll sing on.

124. The King of glory

Rev. W.F. Jabusch

Traditional Israeli folk song
Arr. Betty Pulkingham

Well accented

Refrain
Em
C
The King of glory comes, the nation re-

Em
joi - ces. O - pen the gates be - fore him,

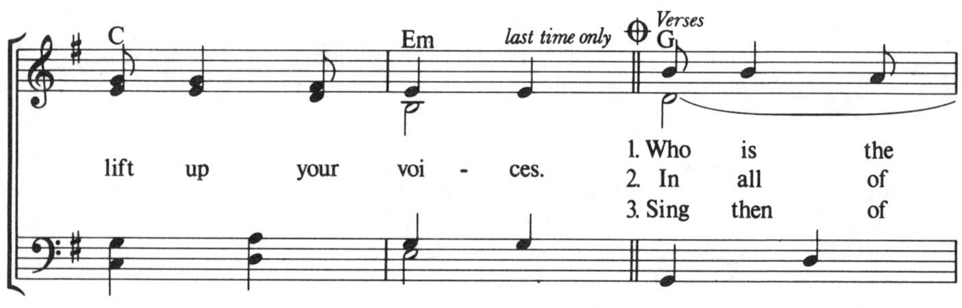

C
Em
last time only
Verses
G
lift up your voi - ces.
1. Who is the
2. In all of
3. Sing then of

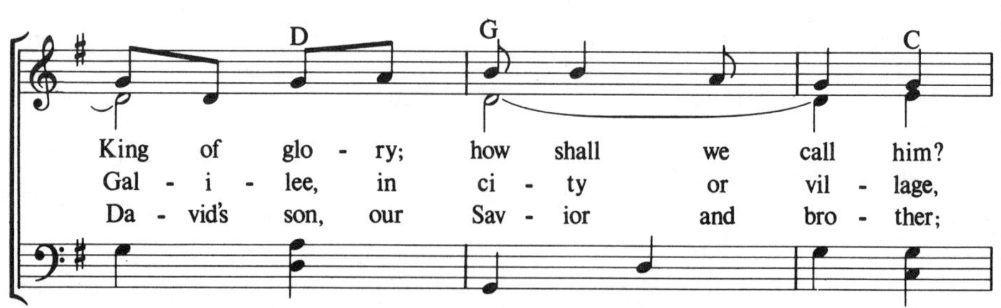

D
G
C
King of glo - ry; how shall we call him?
Gal - i - lee, in ci - ty or vil - lage,
Da - vid's son, our Sav - ior and bro - ther;

G
D
G
B7
He is Em - man - u - el, the pro - mised of a - ges.
he goes a - mong his peo - ple cur - ing their ill - ness.
in all of Gal - i - lee was nev - er an - oth - er.
Em
C
The King of glo - ry comes, the na -
Am
E
tion re - joi - - - - - ces.

4. He gave his life for us, the pledge of salvation.
He took upon himself the sins of the nation.

5. He conquered sin and death; he truly has risen,
And he will share with us his heavenly vision.

125. The foot washing song

Adapted from John 13

Shirley Lewis Brown
Arr. R. J. Batastini

Gracefully
Refrain
C
C
Put on the a - pron of hu - mil - i - ty;
F
C
G
C
serve your broth - er, wash his feet, that he may walk in the
C
F
G
C
way of the Lord, re - freshed, re - freshed.

Verses (may be sung as solo)
C
Am
F
G
C
1. At the last sup - per with his dis - ci - ples Je - sus rose from the ta - ble,
2. When Je - sus knelt be - fore him, Pe - ter said, 'Lord, do you wash my feet?'
Still pro - test - ing, Pe - ter said, 'Lord, you must nev - er wash my feet.'
3. Then said Pe - ter, 'Lord, not on - ly my feet, but al - so my hands and my head.'
4. Then said Je - sus, 'Do you know what it is that I have done?
If I then, your mas - ter and Lord, have stooped to wash your feet,
5. No man is great - er than his mas - ter, no mes - sen - ger than he who sent him.
(humming parts)

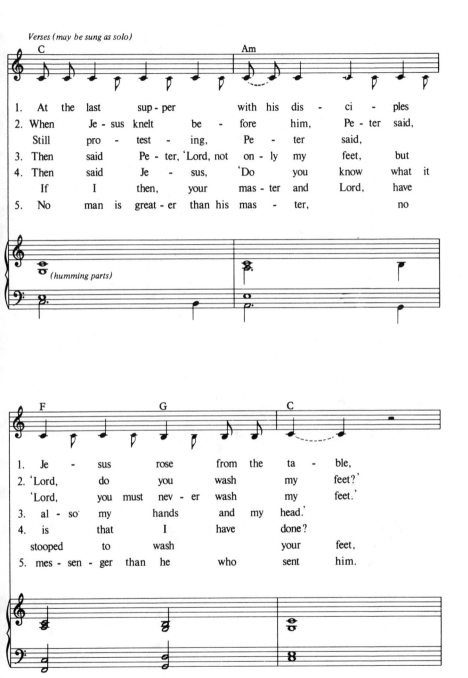

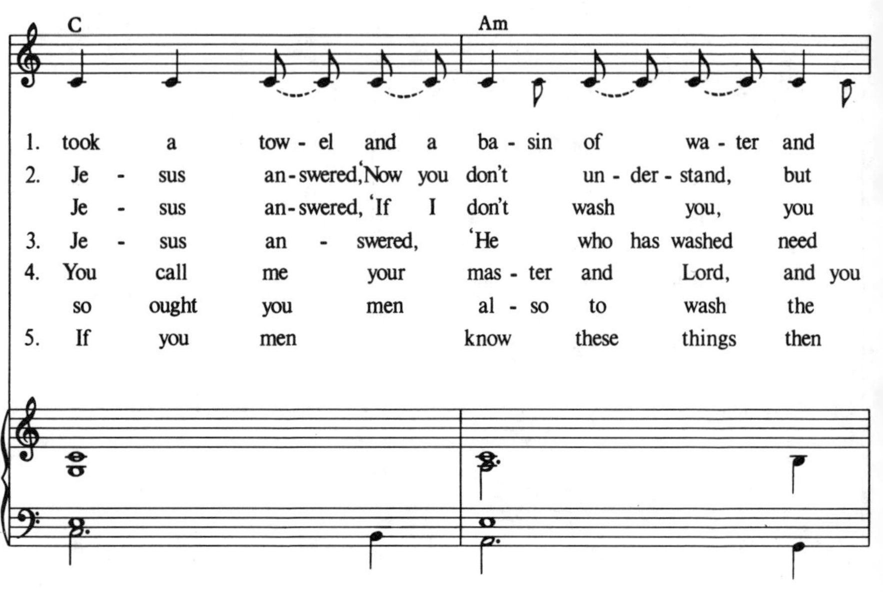
C
Am
1. took a tow - el and a ba - sin of wa - ter and
2. Je - sus an - swered,'Now you don't un - der - stand, but
Je - sus an - swered, 'If I don't wash you, you
3. Je - sus an - swered, 'He who has washed need
4. You call me your mas - ter and Lord, and you
so ought you men al - so to wash the
5. If you men know these things then

F
G
C
1. stooped to wash their feet.
2. la - ter on you will.'
have no part of me.'
3. on - ly wash his feet.'
4. speak the truth, for so I am.
feet of one an - oth - er.
5. hap - py are you if you do them.'

126. Were you there?

North American Spiritual

With deep reverence
1. Were you there when they cru - ci - fied my Lord? Were you there when they cru - ci - fied my Lord?
2. Were you there when they nailed him to the tree? Were you there when they nailed him to the tree?
3. Were you there when they laid him in the tomb? Were you there when they laid him in the tomb?
Oh!
some-times it caus - es me to tremble, tremble, tremble.
Were you there when they cru - ci - fied my Lord?
Were you there when they nailed him to the tree?
Were you there when they laid him in the tomb?

128. Thine be the glory

Edmond Louis Budry
Tr. Richard Birch Hoyle

'Maccabaeus'
George Frederick Handel

With great dignit
1. Thine be the glo - ry, ri - sen, con - q'ring Son,
2. Lo, Je - sus meets us, ri - sen, from the tomb!
3. No more we doubt thee, glo - rious prince of life;
End - less is the vic - t'ry thou o'er death hast won;
Lov - ing - ly he greets us, scat - ters fear and gloom;
Life is nought with - out thee: aid us in our strife;
An - gels in bright rai - ment rolled the stone a - way,
Let the church with glad - ness hymns of tri - umph sing,
Make us more than con - q'rors, through thy death - less love;
Kept the fold - ed grave - clothes, where thy bo - dy lay.
For her Lord now liv - eth, death hath lost its sting.
Bring us safe through Jor - dan to thy home a - bove.

Song number 127 has been deleted from this edition inasmuch as the copyright holder has declined to grant the publishers permission for its continued use.

Thine be the glo - ry, ris - en, con-q'ring Son,

End - less is the vic - t'ry thou o'er death hast won!

129. # Hallelujah today!

Charles Wesley

Betty Pulkingham

Medium rock tempo
Am Em Am
1. Christ the Lord is ri - sen to - day:
2. Love's re - deem - ing work is done;
3. Lives a - gain our glo - rious King!
F Em Am
Sons of men and an - gels say,
Fought the fight, the bat - tle won; Hal - le -
Where, O death, is now your sting?
G Am G Am G
lu - jah! Hal - le - lu - jah! Hal - le - - -
Am
- lu - jah to - day!

G D
Raise your joys and tri - umphs high;
Death in vain for - bids him rise;
Once he died our souls to save;
G D
Sing, you hea - vens and you earth re - ply,
Christ has o - pened par - a - dise,
Where is your vic - to - ry, O grave?
Am G Am
Hal - - - le - - lu -
- jah!
Am *final ending* Em A
Christ the Lord is ri - sen to - day!

4. Soar we now where Christ has led
Following our exalted Head. Hallelujah!
Made like him, like him we rise,
Ours the cross, the grave, the skies. Hallelujah!

130. Christ the Lord is risen today

Tr. Tate and Brady
verse 4: Charles Wesley

'Easter Hymn'
from Lyra Davidica
Descant. Betty Pulkingham

Triumphantly

Optional descant (voice or trumpet
Hal - le - lu, Ha - le - lu - jah!
1. Christ the Lord is risen to - day:
2. Love's re - deem - ing work is done;
3. Lives a - gain our glo - rious King!

Hal - - le - lu - jah! Hal - le -
Hal - - - le - lu - jah!
Sons of men and
Fought the fight, the
Where, O death, is

- lu, Hal - le - lu - jah! Hal - - le - lu - jah!
an gels say, -
bat - tle won, - Hal - - - le - lu - jah!
now thy sting? -
Hal - le - lu, Hal - le - lu - jah!
Raise your joys and tri - umphs high;
Death in vain for - bids him rise,
Once he died our souls to save,

Hal-le - lu - jah! Hal-le- lu, Hal-
Sing ye heav'ns; thou
Hal - - le - lu - jah! Christ hath op - ened
Where thy vic - to -

- le - lu - jah! Hal - le - lu - jah!
earth re - ply,
par - ra - dise,
-ry, O grave?
Hal - - le - lu - - jah!

Soar we now where Christ has led,
Following our exalted Head:
Made like him, like him we rise;
Ours the cross, the grave, the skies;
Hallelujah!

131. He will fill your hearts today

Refrain: Mrs. C. H. Morris
Verses: Betty Pulkingham

Arr. Betty Pulkingham

Skipping along
Refrain
He will fill your hearts to-day to ov - er - flow - ing, as the
Lord comman - ded you, 'bring your ves - sels, not a few,' he will
fill your hearts to-day to ov - er - flow - ing with his
Ho - ly Ghost and power.

1. When the day of Pen - te - cost had come, the be -
2. Suddenly a noise from the sky, which
3. Then they looked up and saw, they
All of them were filled with the Ho - ly Ghost, with the
liev - ers were gath - erd to - geth - er, were
soun - ded like a strong wind blow - ing, a
saw what looked like tongues of fire,
Ho - ly Ghost and power. They be -

gath - er'd to - geth - er in one place, of one
strong wind blow - ing by, filled the whole
tongues of fire spread-ing out, to each
- gan to speak in oth - er lan - gua - ges, in oth - er
mind as the Lord had com - mand - ed.
place, the noise kept on grow - ing.
one, spread - ing out to all the peo - ple.
languages he gave them in that hour!

132. Come, Holy Ghost

Traditional

With dignity and breadth
1. Come, Ho - ly Ghost cre - a - tor blest, Vouchsafe with - in our souls to rest; Come with thy grace and heav'nly aid, And fill the hearts which thou hast made, And fill the hearts which thou hast made.
2. To thee the com - fort - er we cry; To thee the gift of God most high; The fount of life, the fire of love, The soul's a - noint - ing from a - bove, The soul's a - noint - ing from a - bove.
3. The sev'n-fold gifts of grace are thine, O fin - ger of the hand de - vine. True pro-mise of the Fa - ther thou, Who dost the tongue with speech en - dow, Who dost the tongue with speech en - dow.

4. Thy light to every sense impart,
   And shed thy love in every heart;
Thine own unfailing might supply,
   To strengthen our infirmity.

5. Drive far away our ghostly foe,
   And thine abiding peace bestow;
If thou be our preventing guide,
   No evil can our steps betide.

133. Planted wheat

Jeff Cothran

'Hashual'
Traditional Hebrew Melody
Arr. Jeff Cothran

Introduction
Simply and lightly
Recorder and voices; Noo Noo Noo

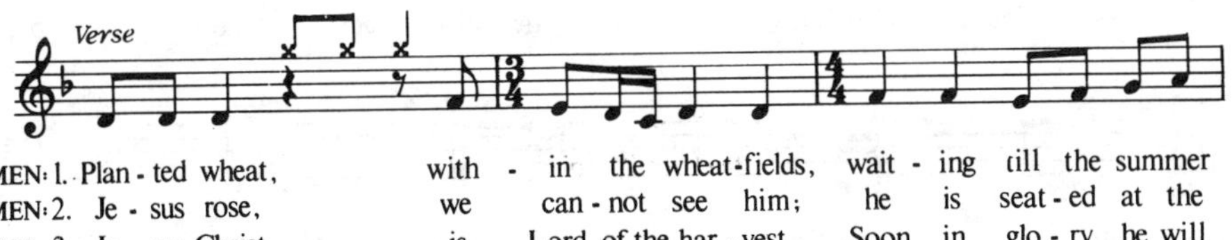

Verse
MEN: 1. Plan - ted wheat, with - in the wheat-fields, wait - ing till the summer
MEN: 2. Je - sus rose, we can - not see him; he is seat - ed at the
ALL: 3. Je - sus Christ is Lord of the har - vest. Soon in glo - ry he will

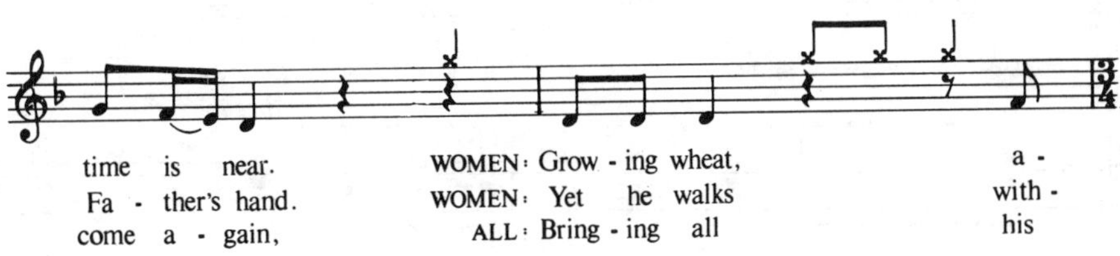

time is near. WOMEN: Grow - ing wheat, a -
Fa - ther's hand. WOMEN: Yet he walks with -
come a - gain, ALL: Bring - ing all his

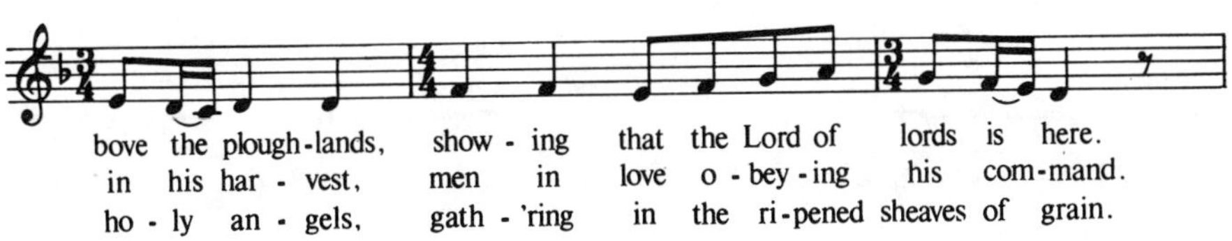

bove the plough-lands, show - ing that the Lord of lords is here.
in his har - vest, men in love o - bey - ing his com-mand.
ho - ly an - gels, gath - 'ring in the ri-pened sheaves of grain.

* Wood block or finger cymbals

Refrain
S
A
T
B
He comes to grow a new cre - a - tion, call - ing out a ho - ly na - tion,
Noo
Noo
He comes to grow a new cre - a - tion, call - ing out a ho - ly na - tion,
2nd. time
all who will be - lieve, and all who will re - ceive. He
Noo Noo Noo Noo Noo Noo
all who will be - lieve, and all who will re - ceive. He

Title and First Line Index

The first line of a piece is included, in italic type, only where it differs from the title.

A new commandment 108
Alleluia 49
Alleluia, alleluia, give thanks 12
Alleluia No. 1 12
Alleluia! Sing to Jesus 96
Alleluia! Sons of God, arise! 146
Amazing grace 18
And can it be? 142
Angel voices ever singing 30
As a doe 174
At the cross 107
At the name of Jesus (2 tunes) 76, 78

Behold, how good and how pleasant it is 165
The bell song 92
Bless thou the Lord 182
Blow, thou cleansing wind 98
The body song 196
The butterfly song 188
By your stripes 94

Calypso carol 210
The canticle of the gift 13
Christ the Lord is risen today 232
Christ the Lord is risen today 230
Come and go with me 147
Come, Holy Ghost, creator blest 238
Complete in him 124

Day by day (2 tunes) 64, 65
Dear Lord and Father of mankind 91

Father, we adore you 49
Fear not, rejoice and be glad 100
The footwashing song 224
The fullness of the Godhead 124

Give me oil in my lamp 16
Glorious things of thee are spoken (2 tunes) 116, 118
Glory be to Jesus 111
Go forth and tell 161
Go tell everyone 156
Go tell it on the mountain 216
God and man at table are sat down 100
God has called you 120
God has spoken 160
God himself is with us 44
God is building a house 102
God is working his purpose out 154
God's spirit is in my heart 156

Hail, thou once despised Jesus 133
Hallelujah! Jesus is Lord! 33
Hallelujah today! 230
He is Lord 48
He shall teach you all things 72
He will fill your hearts today 235
Here comes Jesus 84
Hey, (name), do you love Jesus? 192
Ho! everyone that thirsteth 148
The Holy Ghost medley 126
Holy, holy 40
How firm a foundation 122
How sweet the name 82

I am the bread of life 108
I have decided to follow Jesus 131
I heard the Lord 140
I rejoiced when I heard them say 184
I want to live for Jesus every day 71
I want to walk as a child of the light 60
I want to walk with Jesus Christ 80
I will sing, I will sing 22
If I were a butterfly 188

If the eye say to the hand 196
In Christ there is no east or west 62
Jesus 99
Jesus Christ is alive today 34
Jesus gave her water 126
Jesus is a friend of mine 201
Jesus is Lord 136
Jesus, Jesus is my Lord 190
Jesus, Jesus, wonderful Lord 56
Jesus, never have I heard a name 55
Joy in the Lord 164
The joy of the Lord 138

The King of glory 216
The King of love my shepherd is 115
The kingdom of God 99
Kum ba yah 73

Let all that is within me 42
Let us give thanks 23
Let your light shine 218
The Lord has done great things 168
The Lord has put a new song 171
Lord, I want to be a Christian 63
The Lord is my shepherd 191
Lord of all hopefulness 75
The Lord's my shepherd 178

Morning has broken 26

O Breath of Life 74
O for a thousand tongues 36
Oh! how good is the Lord 20
Oh, how I love Jesus 192
O Lord, all the world belongs to you 151
Oh, Mary, don't you weep 212
Oh, the blood of Jesus 106
Oh welcome, all ye noble saints of old 110
Oh! What a gift 13
O Zion, haste 158
On Jordan's bank 209

Peace is flowing 153
Planted wheat 239
Praise him 32
Praise the Lord 195
Praise to the Lord, the almighty 28
Put on the apron of humility 224
Reach out and touch the Lord 70
Rejoice in the Lord always 27

The sea walker 150
See, amid the winter snow 214
See him a'lying on a bed of straw 210
See the conqueror 132
Seek ye first 99
Silver and gold 88
Sing a new song to the Lord 180
Sing, sing, praise and sing 195
Something in my heart 15
Son of God 43
Spirit divine 58
Spirit of the living God 54

Take my hand and follow me 150
Thank you, Lord 200
Thank you, thank you, Jesus (2 versions) 38, 50
There is a balm in Gilead 90
Thine be the glory 228
This is my commandment 114
This is the day 31
Thou art worthy 52

Wake up! 206
We love the Lord 198
We really want to thank you, Lord 112
We see the Lord 46
The wedding banquet 202
Were you there? 227
Wondrous love 220

You gotta have love in your heart 92

Topical Index

ADORATION (See Worship)

BODY OF CHRIST (See Kingdom)

CHILDREN'S SONGS

The body song
The butterfly song
Give me oil in my lamp
God is building a house
Here comes Jesus
I want to live for Jesus every day
Jesus is a friend of mine
Jesus, Jesus is my Lord
Let your light shine
The Lord is my Shepherd
Oh, how I love Jesus
Praise the Lord
Thank you, Lord
Silver and gold
Something in my heart
Wake up!
We love the Lord
The wedding banquet

FAITH AND VICTORY

Alleluia No. 1
And can it be?
At the cross
Blow, thou cleansing wind
The canticle of the gift
Christ the Lord is risen today
Complete in him
Glory be to Jesus
God has called you
Hail, thou once despised Jesus
The Holy Ghost medley
How firm a foundation
I have decided to follow Jesus
I heard the Lord
Jesus is Lord
Jesus, Jesus is my Lord
The joy of the Lord
Oh, Mary, don't you weep
Planted wheat
See the conqueror

GROWTH AND MATURITY (See Wholeness)

HEALING (See Wholeness)

HOLY COMMUNION (See Kingdom)

HOPE AND VISION

At the name of Jesus (2 tunes)
Day by day (2 tunes)
Fear not, rejoice and be glad
He shall teach you all things
I am the bread of life
I want to walk as a child of the light
In Christ there is no east or west
The King of glory
Lord, I want to be a Christian
The Lord is my shepherd
Lord of all hopefulness
O Breath of Life
Reach out and touch the Lord
We love the Lord

KINGDOM

Alleluia! Sing to Jesus
Alleluia! Sons of God, arise!
A new commandment

At the cross (Holy Communion)
Behold, how good (Psalm 133)
Blow, thou cleansing wind
The body song
Come and go with me
Fear not, rejoice and be glad
The footwashing song
Glorious things of thee are spoken
Glory be to Jesus (Holy Communion)
God and man at table are sat down (Holy Communion)
God is building a house
I am the bread of life (Holy Communion)
I rejoiced when I heard them say (Psalm 122)
The King of love my shepherd is (Holy Communion)
The kingdom of God
Oh, the blood of Jesus (Holy Communion)
Seek ye first
Spirit divine
This is my commandment
We love the Lord
We really want to thank you, Lord

MISSION (See Outreach)

OUTREACH

Alleluia! Sons of God, arise!
Blow, thou cleansing wind
Come and go with me
Go forth and tell
Go tell everyone
Go tell it on the mountain
God has spoken
God is working his purpose out
Ho! everyone that thirsteth
I have decided to follow Jesus
I want to walk with Jesus Christ
The Lord has put a new song (Psalm 40)
O Lord, all the world belongs to you
On Jordan's bank
O Zion, haste
Peace is flowing
The sea walker
Wake up!

PRAISE AND THANKSGIVING

Alleluia No. 1
Alleluia! Sing to Jesus
Amazing grace
Angel voices ever singing
At the name of Jesus (2 tunes)
The bell song
The canticle of the gift
Give me oil in my lamp
Glorious things of thee are spoken (2 tunes)
Glory be to Jesus
Hail, thou once despised Jesus
Hallelujah! Jesus is Lord!
I will sing, I will sing
Jesus Christ is alive today
Jesus is Lord
Joy in the Lord (Psalm 100)
Let us give thanks
The Lord has put a new song (Psalm 40)
Morning has broken
O for a thousand tongues
Oh! how good is the Lord
Praise him
Praise to the Lord, the almighty
Silver and gold
Something in my heart
Thank you, thank you, Jesus
Thine be the glory
This is the day
Thou art worthy
Wake up!
We really want to thank you, Lord

PSALMS

As a doe (Psalm 42)
Behold, how good and how pleasant it is (Psalm 133)
Bless thou the Lord (Psalm 103)
I rejoiced when I heard them say (Psalm 122)
Joy in the Lord (Psalm 100)
The Lord has done great things (Psalm 126)
The Lord has put a new song (Psalm 40)
The Lord's my shepherd (Psalm 23)
Sing a new song to the Lord (Psalm 98)

SEASONAL SONGS

Advent
On Jordan's bank
Wake up!

Christmas
Calypso carol
Oh, Mary, don't you weep
See, amid the winter snow

Epiphany
Go tell it on the mountain
God has spoken
Let your light shine

Passiontide
At the cross (Good Friday)
The footwashing song (Maundy Thursday)
The King of glory (Palm Sunday)
Were you there? (Good Friday)
Wondrous love (Good Friday)

Easter
Alleluia No. 1
The canticle of the gift
Christ the Lord is risen today (2 tunes)
Jesus Christ is alive today
Thine be the glory

Ascension
Alleluia! Sing to Jesus
See the conqueror
We see the Lord

Pentecost
Come, Holy Ghost
Fear not, rejoice and be glad
He will fill your hearts today

Harvest
Planted wheat

WHOLENESS

Amazing grace
The bell song
Bless thou the Lord (Psalm 103)
The body song
By your stripes
Complete in him
Dear Lord and Father of mankind
God has called you
Here comes Jesus
Ho! everyone that thirsteth
How sweet the name
I am the bread of life
I want to walk with Jesus Christ
The joy of the Lord
The King of love
Oh, oh, oh, how good is the Lord
Oh, the blood of Jesus
Planted wheat
Silver and gold
There is a balm in Gilead

WORSHIP

All of my life
Alleluia
As a doe (Psalm 42)
Come, Holy Ghost, creator blest
Father, we adore you
God himself is with us
Holy, holy
How sweet the name
I want to walk as a child of the light
Jesus
Jesus, Jesus, wonderful Lord
Jesus, never have I heard a name
The King of love
Let all that is within me
Oh, the blood of Jesus
Son of God
Spirit divine
Spirit of the living God
Thank you, thank you, Jesus
Thou art worthy
We see the Lord
We love the Lord
Were you there?

Choirmaster's Guide

The following are appropriate for *CHOIRS:*

Alleluia (4 part)
As a doe (unison)
Day by day (unison & 4 part with optional descant)
God and man at table (unison)
God himself is with us (4 part)
He shall teach you all things (2 part)
How sweet the name (unison)
I am the bread of life (4 part)
I want to walk as a child of the light (4 part)
Jesus (4 part)
Jesus, never have I heard a name (4 part)
Joy in the Lord (unison & 4 part)
The King of love (4 part)
Let your light shine (trebles)
Lord, I want to be a Christian (4 part)
Morning has broken (4 part)
Spirit of the living God (4 part)
Were you there? (4 part)

The following hymns have *descants:*

Alleluia! Sing to Jesus
Amazing grace
At the name of Jesus
Christ the Lord is risen today
Glory be to Jesus
Hail, thou once despised Jesus
The Lord's my shepherd (Ps. 23)
See the conqueror

The following songs have verses which may be sung as *SOLOS* or by *SOLO ENSEMBLES:*

Alleluia No. 1
Behold, how good and pleasant it is (Ps. 133)
Bless thou the Lord
Behold, how good (Ps. 133)
The canticle of the gift
Day by day
Fear not, rejoice
The footwashing song
Go tell everyone
Go tell it on the mountain
God and man at table are sat down
He will fill your hearts
I rejoiced when I heard them say (Ps.122)
Jesus, Jesus is my Lord
Let us give thanks
The Lord has done great things (Ps. 126)
The Lord has put a new song (Ps. 40)
Oh, Mary, don't you weep
There is a balm in Gilead
Wake up!
The wedding banquet

The following are *ROUNDS:*

Father, we adore you
God is working his purpose out
He shall teach you all things
The Lord is my shepherd
Rejoice in the Lord always
Seek ye first